"Imagine That!" by Jeff Katzman, age 12

"Imagination is more important

than knowledge."

—Albert Einstein

Special Note to Teachers

We encourage teachers to duplicate the
poems and illustrations in this book.
Children will enjoy having their own
copies to read, color, and design. Each
child may keep an individual collection of
the poems in a folder or booklet.

The pages containing the illustrated
poems have been designed in such a way
that they may be easily reproduced by a
copier. Once a master has been made, the
materials may be duplicated for an entire
class. If the poems are used to motivate
children's original drawings, the
illustrations accompanying the poems
may be blocked with masking tape or a
blank sheet of paper.

IMAGINE THAT!

Illustrated Poems and Creative Learning Experiences

JOYCE KING
Brentwood Art Center

CAROL KATZMAN
Beverly Hills
Unified School District

Illustrated by
DINAH JAMES

Goodyear Publishing Company, Inc.
Santa Monica, California

Library of Congress Cataloging in Publication Data

King, Joyce.
  Imagine that!

  Bibliography: p. 166
  1. Creative thinking (Education) 2. Poetry—Study
and teaching. 3. Creative activities and seat work.
I. Katzman, Carol, joint author. II. Title.
LB1062.K47   372.6'4   75-19569
ISBN 0-87620-410-8

Library of Congress Catalog Card Number: 75-19569

ISBN: 0-87620-410-8

Y-4108-0

Current Printing (last number):
10 9 8 7 6

Printed in the United States of America

Original poems by Joyce King

Editor: Victoria Pasternack
Designer: Einar Vinje

for:

Danny

Janna

Jeffrey

Jon

Kari

Stephanie

and Tali

Contents

Acknowledgments

We have a tremendous feeling of gratitude for the following people, who had a direct hand in creating the pages of this book:

Dave Grady, whose imagination gave us a beginning;

Victoria Pasternack, for her support and care beyond the job of editing;

Einar Vinje, for his elegant design and special interest from cover to cover;

Walther Puffer, principal, and the staff and children of Beverly Vista School, Beverly Hills Unified School District, for their support and participation;

Ed Buttwinick, director, and the staff and children of the Brentwood Art Center, for their support and participation;

Joan Vaupen, assistant art supervisor, Santa Monica Unified School District, for her suggestions and enthusiastic support;

Maria and Jack Pounders, for offering an endless reservoir of resources;

Emily Selwyn and Barbara Smith, whose typing skills untangled the words and letters in the manuscript;

Claire Comiskey, who provided a unique insight into the world of publishing;

The offices of Weinstock and Sinn, for offering us coffee, solitude, and space;

Our special families and friends, whose interest provided a vital source of enthusiasm, motivation, and encouragement;

Jeff, Jerry, and John, for helping us share all the feelings between the lines!

Preface:
Circle of Sharing

Children created this book and we translated it into
a teaching device. The poems were written by
listening to children share their unique feelings and
fantasies in actual classroom situations. The
illustrations were designed to add visual imagery.
The activities were devised to extend the meaning
of the poems by encouraging children to explore,
experience, and discover for themselves. The book is
a circle of sharing. The poems and illustrations
motivate the learning experience, which becomes for
the child an exciting new adventure. As he becomes
involved with the language of the poem, the result is
often the creation of a new poem written by an
inspired, self-directed child.

When poetry and art are used as teaching aids, a
child's curiosity is ignited, and imaginative thinking
and feeling follow. Because of the positive responses
we have observed from both children and teachers,
we would like to expand our circle of sharing to
include you, your children, and your classroom.

Creative Lesson Planning

Sunday night
Feeling blue
Five school days
What to do?

MONDAY

Paper towel rolls and egg cartons turned into fantasy castles and flying machines.

TUESDAY

Scraps of wood and bottle tops turned into "boogle houses," caves, and magic machines.

WEDNESDAY

3"x5" file cards turned into a treasure chest of secret wishes, dreams, and mysteries.

THURSDAY

A large piece of paper, a pencil, and a sentence turned into a written excursion to India, an enchanted birthday party, and a rocket blast to the moon.

FRIDAY

A piece of cardboard, an electric skillet, and a bean sprout turned into a special restaurant with menus and checks, a health food store, and a snack stand with tasty international treats.

Introduction:
Designing the Creative Experience

How can everyday teaching in language and art
become a creative learning experience in your
classroom? The point of this book is to provide the
classroom teacher with the necessary tools to
stimulate the development of creativity in children.
Creative learning takes place when children are
given the time and opportunity to explore and
discover for themselves. Encouraging children to
express their ideas and feelings freely is a vital
factor in promoting creative learning. Accepting and
respecting a child's personal thoughts and his
imagination are equally essential ingredients. We
assist children in their learning development by
questioning them, not by telling them.

A creative environment in the classroom is child
centered and recognizes children's individual needs.
It offers a wide variety of materials to select from
and permits children to move about and experiment
easily. The creative teacher presents new ways for
using traditional materials. He or she emphasizes the
process rather than the final product.

MOTIVATION: THE ILLUSTRATED POEMS

The poems and illustrations serve as instant
motivation in the classroom, inspiring children to
relate what they see and hear to their own natural

imaginations. The poems create graphic images in the reader's mind. The illustrations give the poems visual reinforcement. A poem may be used at a "teachable moment" to directly reinforce a situation or experience that has occurred in the classroom. Or if the teacher finds that there's five minutes left before recess and wonders, "What can I do?"—the poems can be used as a refreshing assistance in preventing lost teaching time. Teachers are frequently heard to cry, "It is mind-boggling to think of continuing this pace . . . dreaming up new and creative projects every week!" By introducing the poems, which motivate and reinforce the coordinated learning activities, youngsters will be creatively involved throughout the school year.

Some of the illustrated poems are presented without accompanying learning activities. This is done to emphasize the importance of helping children develop an appreciation for poetry and art as pleasurable experiences in themselves. A sensitive teacher will quickly realize that children can "turn off" their love for poetry if it is continually used as a motivation for work.

The Poems as Motivation for Children's Drawings

Many of the poems in this book have been used effectively to motivate children's drawings. We suggest that the illustrations accompanying the poems not be shown before children draw their own pictures. In this way, their individuality will not be inhibited and their expressions will be original. Samples of children's drawings at various age levels are reproduced throughout the text.

"Floating Clouds" by Danny King, age 5½

INTEGRATING THE CREATIVE EXPERIENCES

The purpose of the Creative Experiences is to stimulate curiosity and enthusiasm for learning. The experiences strengthen and support the teaching of the poems. The images created by the poems expand when children experiment with various styles of poetry, creative writing, vocabulary building, arts and crafts processes, and stimulating follow-up activities. A wide variety of experiences is suggested. Relating activities from many areas encourages and reinforces the development of new concepts.

Learning to appreciate poetry requires oral language experiences. The following suggestions for providing these experiences may prove helpful to the teacher.

1. Read a poem more than once, slowly and carefully.
2. To build vocabulary, keep a good dictionary handy and refer to it frequently.
3. When reading the poem aloud, read it very slowly and clearly. The sense of poetry is conveyed through the sounds of the words as well as through their meanings. Poetry is meant to be heard.
4. Pay careful attention to what the poem is saying. Make sure that the rhymes and rhythms of the poem do not obscure its meaning for the children.

Effective learning does not occur in pockets of isolated tasks but acquires new meaning in combination with a multitude of integrated activities. These activities are the ingredients that heighten the child's awareness of his world.

Starters and Stretchers

Each set of Creative Experiences begins with Starters and Stretchers, which set the wheels in motion for expanding learning beyond reading the poems. These ideas start the children's thinking processes and stretch their imaginations to new levels of creative expression. They may be used as story openers for creative writing or as kick-offs to motivate expression.

Extenders

The Creative Experiences continue with Extenders, which carry the creative process farther by emphasizing activities in the areas of language and art. In addition, they contain projects, games, and learning center ideas for use in social science, math, and psychomotor activities. The Extenders suggest specific ways for using the tear sheets in the last section of this book.

Suggested Source Books

The Creative Experiences often conclude with a list of classroom-tested source materials and related activities. These may be presented to motivate specific learning experiences described in the text. Additional reference books for teachers and motivational materials for children are included in the Bibliography.

USING THE TEAR SHEETS

The tear sheets are instant materials for teachers to remove from the book, duplicate, and distribute to the children to reinforce specific activities. The tear sheets relate to general themes throughout the text. Some sheets are suggested for use more than once. By taping over the instructions printed on the tear sheets before duplicating them, they become open-ended resources offering limitless possibilities to the creative teacher. For easy removal and use, the tear sheets are perforated and grouped together in Section 4 of this book.

LARGE AND SMALL GROUP INSTRUCTION

Reading the poems is an enjoyable activity for an entire class. Some of the activities that are included are suitable for the class as a whole, while others are designed to meet the needs of small groups. Only the classroom teacher can diagnose the needs of a particular group of learners and prescribe appropriate activities. The activities presented in this book are meant to help the teacher make such decisions.

LEARNING CENTERS

The teacher can further individualize learning by setting up learning centers, or stations, in the classroom. Many of the experiences suggested in the text are appropriate for use at learning centers. Learning centers encourage children to inquire and explore independently. Children begin to assume responsibility for their own learning. This is the first step toward building self-motivated, self-directed learners.

FORMAT OF THE BOOK

Imagine That! is organized into four major sections, the first three corresponding to traditional courses of study in elementary schools. In Section 1, "Our World around Us," children see the BIG picture. The poems and activities in this section relate to the environmental forces in the child's world. In Section 2, "Our Five Senses," the poems and activities describe sensory experiences through specific references to each of the five senses. Section 3, "Me and My Feelings," places the child in the center of the world, where he learns to identify his values and feelings. The poems and activities offer opportunities to build and strengthen the child's self-concept. Section 4 contains the perforated tear sheets ready for use in the classroom. Finally, the Bibliography lists many references for planning further activities.

Gravity

The planets in their galaxy
Brightly dotted stars I see

In a pattern one by one
Revolving fast around the sun

While the earth is spinning round
I stay firmly on the ground

Gravity keeps me in place
As I spin around in space

1

OUR WORLD AROUND US

As the young child's experience of the world begins to expand, his awareness focuses on all that is around him. The child beginning school takes a large step from the sheltered protection of the home into a complex physical and social environment. For the first time, the child's independence is tested as he learns to survive in this intricate world of many colors, seasons, people, and natural forces.

The poems in this section expose the child to the big world. The activities encourage him to explore and think creatively as he begins each new adventure.

What If?

What if the world came to a stop
Winding down just like a top

No rain
No wind
No shadows
No rivers, lakes, or fountains

No clouds
No fog
No drizzles
No ocean, sand, or mountains

Winding down
　　　　just
　　　　　　like
　　　　　　　　a
　　　　　　　　　　top

What if the world came to a stop?

WHAT IF?

STARTERS AND STRETCHERS

What if you took an imaginary ride on a cloud to:

Nonsense Land
Yellow Land
Tiny Land
Backward Land
Upside-Down Land

What if you traded in your cloud for a magic carpet and continued on to:

Far-Away Land
Space Land
Fantasy Land
Never-Never Land
Dream Land

Is the poem "What If?" real or make-believe? Could it ever happen? Imagine yourself in a world that has stopped. Could you survive? Draw a picture that represents this world.

EXTENDERS

Play with Punctuation

Ask the children to take:

A question mark	An exclamation point
A comma	A period

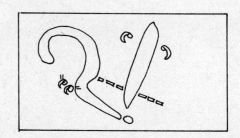

and to scatter the punctuation on their papers. Can they form an interesting design? Add color and small details. Now choose a title for the picture.

Become Weather-Wise

Set up a weather station in the classroom. Ask the children to write daily weather reports. Help them predict the weather for the next twenty-four hours. Using the weather section in the daily newspaper, have the children keep track of the weather in other parts of the country and the world. Ask them to compare and contrast the weather in other cities with their own. How accurate can they be?

People Productions, Inc.

Have children write, produce, and direct their own movie. Use the tear sheet "People Productions, Inc.," on page 171. Have groups of children work together. Children choose a title for the production, a producer, director, cast, screenwriter, cameraperson, location for filming, types of costumes, music, and choreography. The purpose of the tear sheet is to motivate the creation of an actual screenplay. Each group submits a completed tear sheet to the teacher. The teacher may hold a conference with the group and give final approval to the production plans. The completed production could take the form of a play, an operetta, a film, or a slide show.

"Silly Wind" by Lillian Klepa, age 12

Silly Wind

Silly Wind
Stop pushing me
You're not pleasant company

You make me run
And rush about
Your loud shrill whistle
Makes me shout

So go now, Wind
Do be polite
Blow away into the night

Foggy Blanket

The fog came
Rolling in today
Like a blanket
Dark and gray

Through the fog
I tried to peek
Like a game of
Hide and Seek

I wait for it
To disappear
So I can see things
Fresh and clear

Rain Patter

Rain can make everything
Glisten with light
The grass is so green
And the flowers so bright

Rain can make puddles
To walk in and splash
And sometimes the thunder
Will come with a crash

Rain can make noises
Some soft and some loud
And all of it comes from
A big dark gray cloud

Floating Clouds

Up, up high in the sky
A big gray cloud
Came floating by

Bigger, bigger grew the cloud
Then the rain came
Fast and loud

Soon the sun came into view
And turned the sky
From gray to blue

The Sun

The sun shines down
Dim or bright
Lovely sunsets
Bring the night

In the morning
Rays of sun
Warm the land
For work and fun

We need our sun
To help things grow
And people need sunshine
Wherever they go

My Shadow

I have a shadow
It likes to follow me
Jumping and turning
Wherever I may be

Sometimes my shadow
Seems heavy and wide
Then all of a sudden
My shadow will hide

My shadow is with me
Way up in a tree
I like my shadow
It's good company

Shady Spot

I have a very special spot
I go to when the days are hot
Beneath a shady roof of trees
I sit and feel a happy breeze

The Seasons

Summer is the season
For playing and fun
Swimming and hiking
Water and sun

Autumn is the season
For leaves to fall down
Turning from bright green
To orange and brown

Winter is the season
When branches are bare
Snow on the mountains
Frost in the air

Spring is the season
For blossoming out
Fruit trees are blooming
And vegetables sprout

the Seasons

STARTERS AND STRETCHERS

Senses and Seasons. Encourage children to refer to the seasons in relation to their five senses. How does fall:

Look	Smell
Feel	Sound
Taste	

EXTENDERS

More!

Extend the meaning of each season. Read the poem for each season on the following pages.

"Summer Days"
"Snow Wear"
"Autumn's Orchestra"
"I Am Spring"

Seasoning

Divide the class into four teams. Write the name of each season (with plenty of space in between) on the chalkboard. Each team stands in front of one word. At the signal, the first member of each team

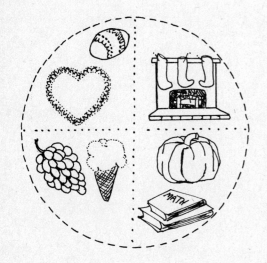

goes to the board and writes one word to describe the season. He comes back and gives his chalk to the next person in line. The relay continues as each player adds one word to the column and hands the chalk to the next person (no repeats). The first team to finish having all its members write a word is the winner. The same exercise can be conducted with students seated at their desks, using paper and pencil.

Design a Mandala of Four Seasons

A *mandala* is a magic circle. It is magic because each child can create his very own. The circle is the first man-made artistic symbol. The first symbol is in the center of the mandala. To make a mandala, cut circles of any size out of a large sheet of art paper. Provide colored markers or oil pastels. Crayons may be used and a watercolor wash applied for a crayon-resist effect. Divide circles into four parts. First draw a symbol of the seasons in the center. It can be a flower, a sun, a leaf, and so on. Now fill in the four sections with colors and symbols that relate to specific seasons.

Examples:

Summer—yellow, bikes, beach
Autumn—brown, orange, fire, school, pumpkins
Winter—blue, snowflakes, skiing
Spring—pastel, colored blossoms, baby animals

Give children the opportunity to design their mandalas any way they wish. Sections can be divided evenly or with irregular lines. Cut out circles. Spray them with clear, glossy spray. Mount them on black paper.

Windowpanes

Use a ruler to divide a large sheet of art paper into four equal sections. Use crayons to depict a different season in each "window." Press hard on the crayons. Now use a watercolor wash to create a windowpane effect.

Trees for All Seasons

Use a large sheet of art paper. Use brown paint or felt-tip marker to draw the trunk and limbs of a tree. Decide on a season appropriate for your tree. Use colored tissue paper squares to depict that season.

> Summer—green leaves, flowers, fruit
> Autumn—orange, red, golden leaves
> Winter—bare limbs, snow falling
> Spring—pink blossoms

Autumn Rubbings

Collect leaves of many shapes, sizes, and colors. Place leaves vein side up under a sheet of newsprint. Using a peeled crayon, rub the side of the crayon over the paper, causing the leaf to leave an impression. Repeat the process using different colors of crayons. (This activity can be used as motivation for more rubbings: carved stone, brick walls, linoleum tiles.)

Cook for All Seasons

Think of foods associated with each season. Plan some appropriate menus and begin cooking in the classroom. Some suggestions to get you started:

> Summer—berries, melons, lemonade
> Autumn—pumpkin pie, fresh cranberries
> Winter—baked apples, hot chocolate
> Spring—garden vegetables for salads

SUGGESTED SOURCE BOOK

Duvoisin, Roger. *House of Four Seasons*. New York: Lothrop, Lee & Shepard, 1956. After reading the story, children will enjoy designing their own houses and choosing a season for the setting.

Summer Days

Black tar stuck on both my feet
Melted ice cream cones to eat

Gritty sand between my toes
Sunburn on my back and nose

Castles crushed beneath the tide
Clouds that force the sun to hide

Bright or dim, sun or haze
How I love those summer days

Snow Wear

Jackets and sweaters
Stockings and boots
Snug hats and mittens
Warm woolen suits

All bundled up
And ready to go
Out of the house
To play in the snow

Although I feel clumsy
In all of these clothes
I am so happy
Whenever it snows

Autumn's Orchestra

Quiet crunchy noises
Autumn twigs and leaves

Rushing whistle noises
Fall wind twirls and weaves

Puffy chimney noises
Cozy fireplace

Gentle rainy noises
Chill takes Autumn's place

I Am Spring

The animals are strolling by
The flowers nod their heads
The trees bring special blossoms
The birds make nests for beds

The clock says daylight savings
The daytime hours are longer
The sun is staying later
The moonbeams come out stronger

The vegetables are sprouting
The wind and rain both sing
The fruits are slowly ripening
The world says "I am Spring"

"I Am Spring" by Rachel Davidson, age 9

Save the Day

Once there was a pretty day
Then it seemed to fade away
Because along the road a man
Left some papers and a can

Then he swiftly drove his car
Spreading smog both near and far
And at his home the trash can grew
Where to put it no one knew

It seems in everybody's haste
The land began to fill with waste
Then the day grew very bitter
Because of all the smog and litter

Now what can we do or say
To try and save the pretty day?

SAVE THE DAY

STARTERS AND STRETCHERS

Vocabulary Building. Find pictures to illustrate each ecology word:

Noise	Trash	Recycle
Smog	Population	Crisis
Waste	Smoke	Pollution
Litter	Energy	(land, sea, air)

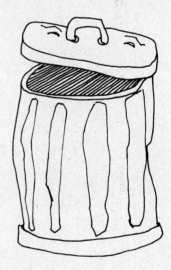

If your trash can could talk, what would it say?
How can you save the pretty day?

At home I fight pollution by _____.
At school I fight pollution by _____.
If I were invited to talk to our school about pollution, I would say _____.

EXTENDERS

Ecologics

Analyze current ecology measures being taken by our country. What is being done to conserve energy and avoid waste? What are the effects of air pollution on our bodies? How is water pollution harmful to sea life? How does land pollution affect our environment? How can families and schools become involved in conserving energy, fighting pollution, and avoiding waste?

Pollution Solutions

After pollution problems have been discussed, ask children to think about specific solutions. How can each child be actively involved in helping to solve pollution problems?

Example: Children collect all the litter found on the school grounds in one day. Create a litter display. Can this litter be recycled and used in a creative way?

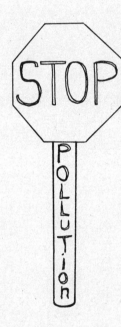

Stop Pollution—A Bulletin Board

Design a replica of a stop sign. Use red paper cut in an octagonal shape. Put it on a bulletin board. Add the word *POLLUTION.* Around the sign include children's suggestions and stories related to fighting pollution.

Measure Noise Pollution

Turn on a tape recorder during a class disturbance. A short time later, play it back for children to hear. This is a most effective and powerful way to demonstrate and measure noise pollution in the classroom.

S.O.S.

Begin your own "Save Our School" program. Have children design S.O.S. posters about fighting pollution, recycling, noise, litter, and waste. Help the whole school become ecology-conscious.

Recycling Station

Ask children to bring small objects from home that are no longer of any use to them. Remind them to ask their parents for permission first. Designate a section of the classroom for the Recycling Station. Feature one item brought from home each day. Encourage children to offer suggestions for reusing the item. After the students have made suggestions, have the class vote to decide who keeps the item, or the whole class could decide to throw the item away.

Many scraps brought from home can be incorporated into art projects:

Collage
Scrap building
Junk sculpture

Garage Sale

Prepare for a real garage sale at school. Have children bring items to school that they wish to sell. Securing adult permission is a good idea. Suggest that the children price their items realistically. The garage sale may be conducted as an auction. Distribute play money to each child. Children may bid on desired items. Or, the sale may be conducted as a lottery. Names of the children are put into a basket. One name is drawn to claim each item. In this way, old things will be recycled.

Strike Up the Band

Create rhythm instruments from materials found at home:

Foil pie plates
Boxes containing pebbles or beans
Bottles and tin cans with utensil beaters

Have children decorate their instruments using materials of their own selection. Use the instruments to clap the rhythm of poems, sentences, names, and class songs.

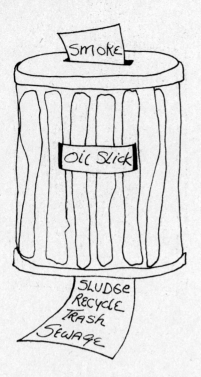

Empty the Trash Can

Make a large game board from colored tagboard. Cut it in the shape of a trash can. Use a marking pen to draw in details. Cut a slit (window) in the lid. Give children strips of tagboard that can be pulled through the slit. Each child writes as many ecology words as he can think of on his strip. Insert the strip into the slit so that it can be pulled back through. Players take turns reading (spelling, defining, giving synonyms or antonyms) each word on the list as it appears in the window. Give one point for each correct pronunciation, definition, etc. Players continue to pull the word list through the window. When the last strip has been pulled through, the player with the most points wins for emptying the trash can first.

Measure "Near" and "Far"

Reread the line, "Spreading smog both near and far," from the poem "Save the Day." Ask each child to define the meaning of *near* and *far*. (There will be different meanings for each child.) Take a class survey to indicate places that are near and far to each child. Compare the results.

Scenes of Pollution

Have children design their own filmstrips. Use blank 35mm film leader. This can be obtained from local film stores. Using grease markers to design their filmstrips, children create scenes depicting various aspects of pollution. Give children opportunities to share and narrate their productions.

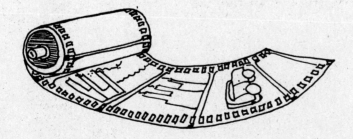

SUGGESTED SOURCE BOOKS

Hurd, Edith Thatcher. *Wilson's World*. New York: Harper and Row, 1964. Children will enjoy hearing the story of Wilson, whose world became so cluttered that finally there was only one word to describe it: "Phooey!!" To extend the learnings in the book, have each child design his own world on a ditto master. Label each child's drawing (for example, "Jane's World"), duplicate, collate, and make individual booklets. Design a cover, "Our World." Each child will enjoy having a booklet of his classmates' drawings. This project could be done as a class art activity. Each child contributes a chalk drawing of his world. Assemble the drawings into a class book.

Madian, Jon. *Beautiful Junk*. Boston: Little, Brown, 1968. This book tells a fictionalized story of the building of the Watts Towers in Los Angeles. Introduce Simon Rodia as the creator of the Watts Towers. Show pictures, films, and arrange a field trip, if possible. Give children an opportunity to build their own Watts Towers. Have children bring in all kinds of junk—nails, tiles, screws, mosaic chips, wire, etc. Provide clay to create a towerlike structure. Children mold their towers and carefully imbed all of their junk materials into the clay. Towers may be wrapped with lengths of fine wire. Encourage imagination in designing these junk towers.

Zion, Gene. *Dear Garbage Man*. New York: Harper and Row, 1957. Stan, the garbage man, runs into a problem in his efforts to recycle the city's garbage. Children will find warmth and humor in the story and also gain some insight into the difficulties of recycling, before they attempt to do it in the classroom.

"Save the Day"
by Stephanie King, age 9

Home

Some houses are big
Some houses are small
Some houses are wide
Some houses are tall

So many houses
Wherever I roam
But the very best one
Is my own special home

HOME

STARTERS AND STRETCHERS

We just moved from (city) to (city) and need to find
a house before school starts. We have (number)
people in our family. We have (number) pets. My
parents like (type) style houses. We have a budget of
(amount). I hope our house will have (attic,
basement, clubhouse, room of my own).

EXTENDERS

House Hunting

Give the children opportunities to construct houses
of their own design using a wide variety of media.

Milk Carton Houses. Children cover cartons of
various sizes with construction paper. From another
sheet of paper, they cut out details and paste them
on with glue.

Stand-up Houses. Children fold a 9″ x 12″ sheet of
construction paper in half. They cut out a house,
leaving a hinge (from the fold) at the top, so that it
can stand. Children decorate the front of the house.
They write on the address. On the inside, they draw
the rooms of the house. On the back, they draw the
family and the activity they enjoy doing together.
The houses can be propped over the backs of chairs
all around the classroom.

Peek-a-boo Houses. Children design a house on a large sheet of drawing paper. They cut out the windows by cutting three sides of each window. The flap remains attached and folds upward. Similarly, the door is cut out along the top and the bottom and one side, folding either to the left or the right. Then, children place another sheet of paper under the house. They trace around the cut-out areas that appear in the windows and the door. Next, children draw small illustrations in these squares to show what is going on inside the house. Finally, they glue the large house on top of the small illustrations. Open the windows and door and PEEK-A-BOO!

Marshmallow Houses. Children build houses with miniature marshmallows and toothpicks by inserting toothpicks into marshmallows and repeating the process. The toothpicks and marshmallows form geometric shapes. Instruct them to build the base first so the house will stand. Make the house big or small, wide or tall. Small, colored gumdrops may be added for interest. Glue the base to a square of cardboard.

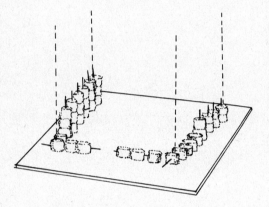

Dough Sculpture Houses. Recipe: Pour 4 cups of flour into a large bowl. Add 2 cups of salt. Mix well with a spoon and add 1¾ cups of water. Mix well and knead with hands for five minutes. Use immediately. (Dough is not good after four hours.) Using a rolling pin, children roll out the dough. They use a tongue depressor to cut out the desired shapes. Work directly on a cookie sheet. Add detail by molding small pieces of dough and applying them with water. Bake in 350° oven for about one hour until hard. Decorate with marking pens. Mount on wood plaque, if desired. Spray with acrylic finish to preserve. Remember: Dough sculpture is *not* edible.

Plywood Houses. Children cut frames out of plywood for each house. Include pointed roof, if desired. Glue or nail together. Paint. Plywood houses are particularly suitable for building a community.

Community Project

Cover several tables (pushed end to end) with butcher paper. Use marking pens to mark off the streets and important buildings in the children's neighborhood. Draw in each child's house in the correct location. Add appropriate landscaping and other community landmarks.

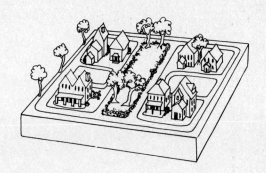

Community Resources

Invite a builder to come to your classroom to speak to the students. Ask him to bring some blueprints for the children to see. Ask him to explain the sequential development in building a house.

Aids to Architecture

Expose children to various styles of architecture:

  Spanish
  Colonial
  English
  Ranch
  Modern-Contemporary
  Futuristic (geodesic)

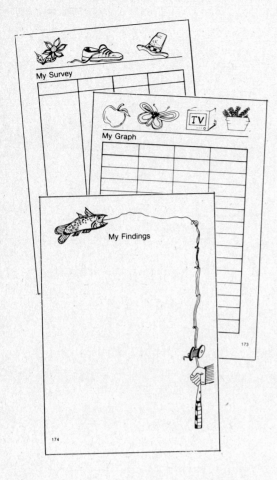

Have children take a survey to discover the different styles of architecture of the houses on their streets and in the community. Use the "My Survey" tear sheet on page 172. Select four styles of architecture and write one style at the top of each column. Use the "My Graph" tear sheet on page 173 to represent the results of the survey. Interpret the results on the "My Findings" tear sheet on page 174. Children can choose an architectural style to illustrate. (For specific instructions for using surveys, graphs, and findings tear sheets, see pages 129–30).

Extra suggestion: Children study famous architects for research projects—for example, Frank Lloyd Wright's Robie House in Chicago, Illinois; Antoni Gaudí's Casa Milá apartment house in Barcelona, Spain; and Le Corbusier's Savoye House in the suburbs of Paris, France.

Hammers and Nails

Houses are made of assorted materials. Collect building materials used in constructing a house:

Wood   Stone   Tile
Brick   Stucco   Clay

Sort and label all of the materials. Discuss how the weather and the geographic region might affect the type of materials used. Use the tear sheet on page 175 to build a "Word House." Think of descriptive words and building materials for a chimney (for example, "brick," "smoke"), roof ("tile," "shake," "shingle"), window ("panes," "glass"), door ("knob," "lock," "wood") and write the words in the appropriate spaces on the tear sheet.

For Sale

Display children's houses that have been constructed from various media. Each child writes a real estate advertisement to sell his house. Children include the following information:

1. Description (size) of the house (how many bedrooms, bathrooms, etc.)
2. Lot size
3. Address
4. Nearest schools

5. Extras (swimming pool, gardens)
6. Price of house
7. OPEN HOUSE times

Each child becomes a real estate broker. Children create FOR SALE signs—any shape, size, or design. When the house is sold, have the buyer and seller sign escrow papers. Place a SOLD sign on the house.

Vocabulary Building: House Talk

Escrow	Mortgage
Broker	Inspection
Foreclosure	Commission
Down Payment	Real Estate

Room Dividers

Make a gameboard from a large sheet of colored tagboard. Cut the gameboard in the shape of a house. Draw each room in the house. Distribute magazines and have children cut out pictures of furniture and household items. Mount the pictures on cards. Children place each picture in the appropriate room of the house. Suggest that the students make a list of as many words as they can think of that relate to each room in the house. The class can work in committees, with each group assigned to a different room. After the lists are compiled, write each word on a small card. Children read one card at a time, placing it on the gameboard in the appropriate room.

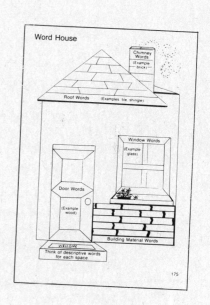

Write a House Book

Use construction paper to cut out the shape of a house. Trace the same shape on several sheets of lightweight paper. Staple the sheets together at the top. Suggest that the children design the cover to represent their own house. Children use the pages inside to tell about their house, draw pictures, and show their family inside the house. Encourage children to write a descriptive sentence on each page. Paste a pocket for a library card on the back cover. Children check out each other's books and sign the cards to show that they have read them.

SUGGESTED SOURCE BOOKS

Duvoisin, Roger. *House of Four Seasons.* New York: Lothrop, Lee and Shepard, 1956. Ask children to choose their favorite season. Make a tissue paper collage with colors appropriate for that season. Use small squares of tissue and apply with starch. Allow the collage to dry completely. Use poster paint to design your house on top of the tissue.

Krauss, Ruth. *A Very Special House.* New York: Harper and Row, 1953. After reading the book, have the children design a special house for "me, Me, ME." Use a shoe box. Paint the inside. Create your own special furniture from pipe cleaners, tongue depressors, or paper cutouts. Use your imagination to design some special animals to live in the house. Cut them out and paste them inside.

Design a "Dream House" of your own. List all of the characteristics of your "Dream House." Build it from a large cardboard carton. Use heavy chipboard to create divisions in the box to represent the rooms. Use pieces of carpet, wallpaper, fabrics to decorate. Paint the outside of the carton.

Montresor, Beni. *House of Flowers, House of Stars.* New York: Alfred A. Knopf, 1962. Children will enjoy reading about all kinds of houses: big, little, happy, unhappy, real, and make-believe. Give children the opportunity to create houses of their own.

"Home" by Jill Gordon, age 8

Palmer, Helen. *Why I Built the Boogle House*. New York: Beginner Books, 1964. After reading the book, children will have many ideas about what a "Boogle" is. Have each child design a house for his own "Boogle," using scraps of wood glued or nailed together. The house might be any shape or size, depending on the child's concept of "Boogle." Make a "Boogle" from pipe cleaners. Place it inside the house. Use a wide variety of colors to paint the finished house. Design individual "Boogle" filmstrips telling of your "Boogle's" home and activities.

"Home" by Carrie Newkirk, age 13

Clockwork

The clock works by numbers
As we watch we can learn
The hands tell the time
While they both move and turn

The first sixty seconds
A minute has passed
Now watch the hand closely
One second goes fast

Then watch the minutes
How long does it take
Sixty whole minutes
An hour to make

In twenty-four hours
Some clocks make a chime
For that's a whole day
And the tone of the time

CLOCKWORK

STARTERS AND STRETCHERS

Children will enjoy making these comparisons
between "kids and clocks." Some suggestions might
include:

They both have faces.
They both have hands.
They both can tell time.
They both can run.
They both make noise.
They both watch the hours.
They both can go around in circles.
They both can be turned on.
They both can be turned off.
They both can stop working, and they both
come in many shapes, sizes, and colors.

EXTENDERS

Go for a Clock Walk

Listen for clock sounds at home and at school. Make
a list of the clock sounds you hear. Some examples
might include:

Ticking	Buzz
Ring (alarm)	Music (clock-radio)
Chime	Click (digital clock)

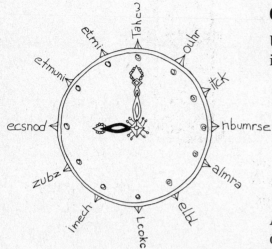

Extra suggestion: Use rhythm instruments to create the clock sounds heard at home and at school.

CLOCK WORDS

Using the drawing of the clock, scramble each word in a different position on the clock's face:

Hour	Buzz
Alarm	Time
Chime	Numbers
Minute	Clock
Tick	Second
Bell	Watch

Ask children to unscramble the words to fix the clock.

Clock Collections

See how many different kinds of clocks and watches you can think of that measure time. Find pictures in magazines and catalogues to illustrate each type of clock. Be sure to include:

Grandfather	Antique
School	Travel clock
Alarm	Stopwatch
Kitchen	Wristwatch
Clock-radio	Picture watch

Mount the pictures on cardboard. Label them and sort them by categories.

Watch a Sundial

The sundial is the oldest known device for showing the time of day. It measures the angle of a shadow cast by the sun on a pointer. Locate a sundial in your community (try parks, museums, and city recreational areas). Encourage children to visit and tell time on these ancient clocks.

Examine an Hourglass

The hourglass also measures time. When were they used? Are they still in use today? Try to locate several types of hourglasses: egg timers, hourglasses, and half-hourglasses.

Timetable for Roman Numerals

Provide opportunities for children to design their own clocks. Set up a timetable center in the classroom. Provide large circles or paper plates for clock faces, brads and short and long strips of construction paper for hands. Have the children use marking pens to draw Roman numerals on the clock face. The hands are attached to the face with brads.

SUGGESTED SOURCE BOOK

Craig, M. Jean. *The Dragon in the Clock Box*. New York: W. W. Norton, 1962. Children will enjoy reading the story of Joshua and his wondrous clock box. After listening to the story, children may design their own clock boxes, creating their own secret treasures to keep inside.

"Clockwork" by Steven O'Dell, age 10

Color Talk

Colors, colors all around
In the sky, on the ground

    Colors of the rainbow
    Colors of the sea
    Colors of the flowers
    Colors of the tree

Sometimes dark, sometimes light
Sometimes dull, sometimes bright

    Red, yellow, and orange
    Purple, green, and blue

When I see a color, I hear it talking, too
What does orange say to you?

Color Talk

STARTERS AND STRETCHERS

Imagine the world in black and white.
What problems would be created in a world of
no color?
What if you woke up one morning and the
whole world was (name one color)?
How would you feel?
Now paint the world another color.
How do different colors make you feel?

EXTENDERS

Tape a Shape

Place lengths of masking tape at different angles
over a masonite board. Use brightly colored poster
paint to color the remaining exposed areas. Allow
time to dry, then pull off the tape. The resulting
design will be interesting geometric shapes of many
colors. This is an illustration of graphic art work
found in famous paintings of Piet Mondrian, Frank
Stella, and Morris Louis.

Color Aid

How do we use color in our daily lives?

1. Safety (traffic lights)
2. Home decorations
3. Clothes
4. Toys
5. Food

Color Talks

Divide a sheet of paper into eight equal sections. Print the name of a color at the top of each square. Each child writes or draws pictures of as many things as he can think of that represent that color. At the conclusion, the students share and compare their lists.

Color Catch

Children form a circle. One child is chosen to hold a ball and stands in the center of the circle. At the signal, the child in the center throws the ball to one child in the circle. As he throws, he calls out a color. As he catches the ball, the child in the circle names an object represented by that color. Then he throws the ball back to the child in the center and calls out another color. The child in the center catches the ball and responds by calling out an object. If the player in the circle fails to name an object, he is eliminated. If the player in the center fails to respond, he changes places with the player in the circle.

Color Fix-Up

Have children bring old, dull, dreary things to school:

    Chair   Lamp base
    Stool   Tool chest
    Shelf

Provide paint and see how color improves them. Parental permission is suggested.

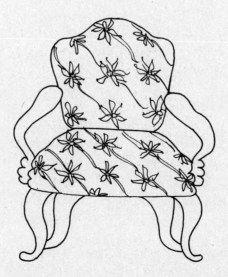

Everything You Always Wanted to Know but Were Afraid to Ask (or Didn't Have Time to Find Out) about Color

The Basic Colors (sometimes called prismatic colors):

Red   Green
Orange   Blue
Yellow   Purple (or Violet)

Note that black and white are not considered colors. In addition, black is considered to represent lack of color, and white represents pure light.

The Primary Colors (arrow points to the center of a color wheel on the accompanying diagram):
Red
Yellow
Blue

The Secondary Colors (arrow points to the outside of the color wheel on the accompanying diagram):
Orange
Purple
Green

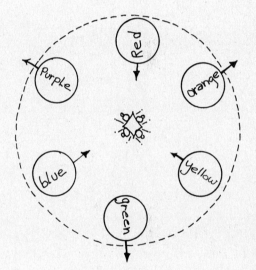

Each secondary color is made by combining the primary colors on both sides of it on the color wheel. (For example, red and yellow make orange.)

The Complementary Colors (colors that are opposite each other on the color wheel):
Red and Green
Blue and Orange
Yellow and Purple

These colors are arranged so that each falls opposite its complement on the color wheel. They are also considered contrasting colors.

Hues:
A secondary color may be combined with the primary color on either side of it to produce a hue. Green and yellow produce a gradation, or hue, of green.

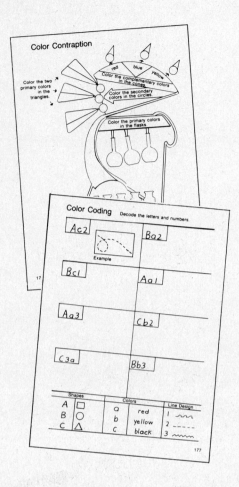

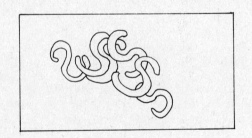

Color Contraptions

Duplicate the "Color Contraption" tear sheet on page 176. Ask students to:

1. Color the basic colors in the bottles.
2. Color the primary colors in the flasks.
3. Color the secondary colors in the circles.
4. Color the two primary colors that combine to make each secondary color in the triangles.
5. Color the complementary, or contrasting, colors in the cones.

Color Coding

Children learn about secret codes. Use the "Color Coding" tear sheet on page 177. Capital letters designate shapes. Lower-case letters represent colors. Numbers indicate line designs. Using the code on the bottom of the tear sheet, children follow the coding and create their own color shape and line design. After children have had experience decoding, suggest that they choose their own letters, numbers, and symbols to write secret codes of their own.

Alphabet Collage

Choose letters of the alphabet. Cut them out of tissue paper. Apply them to art paper with starch. Repeat until the paper is covered with an alphabet collage.

SUGGESTED SOURCE BOOKS

Lionni, Leo. *Little Blue and Little Yellow.* New York: Ivan Obolensky, 1959. Children will enjoy the story of two blobs of paint ("Little Blue" and "Little Yellow") who hug each other until they both turn green. The adventures of these two colors provide an exciting setting for introducing basic color mixing.

O'Neill, Mary. *Hailstones and Halibut Bones.* Garden City, N.Y.: Doubleday, 1961. Illustrated by Leonard Weisgard. Read the book aloud to the class to build an awareness of color in the environment. While reading the book, hold up a sheet of paper of each color, giving the children an opportunity to form color images. As a follow-up activity, ask children to select a color. How do they feel: sad, happy, angry? What image does the color create? Is the color soft or loud? Children will enjoy writing stories and booklets about the feelings created by colors.

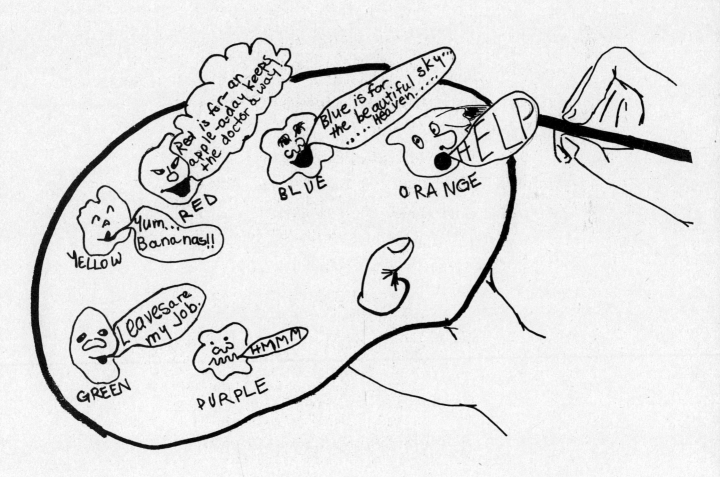

"Color Talk" by Susan Stonefield, age 12½

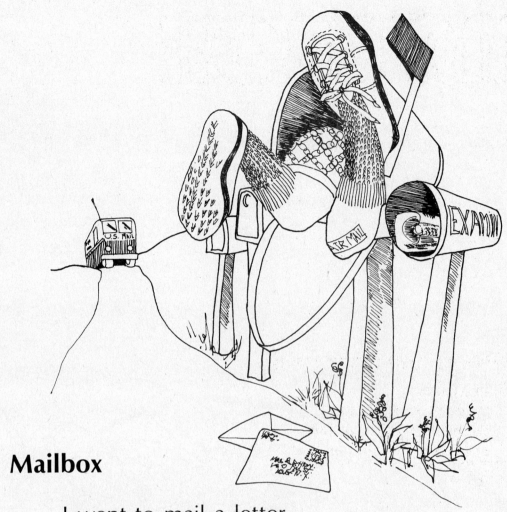

Mailbox

I went to mail a letter
And slid right in the box
All that you could see of me
Were tennis shoes and socks

I self-addressed my elbow
And air-mail stamped my knee
Soon I would be ready
For the next delivery

I folded like an envelope
And in a day or so
I'd go with all the letters
To Japan or Mexico

MAILBOX

STARTERS AND STRETCHERS

I am a letter.
I am going to (address).
I am wearing a (type) stamp.
I have an important message for (name of person).
MAIL ME.

EXTENDERS

Life Cycle of a Letter

Children experiment to find out what happens to a letter after it has been mailed:

1. Self-address an envelope.
2. Write a return address.
3. Place a stamp in the upper right-hand corner.
4. Mail the letter. Keep a record of the day and time mailed.
5. Discuss the different steps involved once the letter is picked up by a postal employee. Letters are stacked, cancelled, sorted, bundled, put on trains and planes, re-sorted at the destination, stored, and finally delivered.

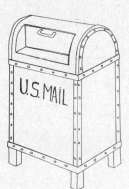

6. Children receive their letters. How long did it take? Ask children to list the steps to the delivery of the letter.

Vocabulary Building: Mail Talk

By using reference books, acquaint children with postal vocabulary. Present the following mail terminology, providing examples whenever possible.

Postcard
Prestamped postage
Cancelled stamps
Parcel Post
General Delivery
Post Office Box (for personal use in post offices)
Collect on Delivery (C.O.D.)
Registered Mail
Insurance
Special Delivery
Wrapping for mailing
Weighing letters and packages to determine cost of postage
Special Handling
Dead Letter Office
Money Order
Classes of mail (first, second, third, and fourth)

If possible, invite a post office employee to talk to the class. Ask him specific questions in advance and suggest that he bring examples to illustrate his talk.

Mail Assortment

Postcard	Package
Letter	Newspaper
Magazine	Catalogue

Discuss differences in cost of postage and length of delivery time for the above-mentioned items.

Mail Carriers

Train	Helicopter
Plane	Truck
Boat	

Discuss which of the above vehicles might be used to deliver mail between two cities or countries. Is it ever necessary to use more than one vehicle to deliver a letter?

Mail Compartments

Cover the outside of a discarded soda bottle carton with contact paper or paint. Label each section with a child's name. Mail compartments offer the teacher and children instant communication. The teacher can write her or his name on one of the compartments. Several boxes can be stacked together, stapled, or nailed.

Address-O-Board

Designate a bulletin board that can be used as the class directory. Give each child a 3″ x 5″ blank index card. Ask the student to write his name (last name first), address, and telephone number on the card. He might also want to draw a thumbnail sketch of himself. Attach all the cards to the bulletin board in alphabetical order by the child's last name.

Address Books

Call your local telephone company. They can usually make available individual paperback address books for each student. If these are not available, small spiral notebooks or composition books can be used. Print a letter of the alphabet on each page. Have the children use the "Address-O-Board" to copy names, addresses, and telephone numbers of their classmates. Be sure they alphabetize the names by writing them on the correct page.

Constructing Mailboxes

Mailboxes come in all shapes and sizes. Use heavy cardboard or lumber for construction. Paint the outside of the box, letter appropriate name of the room and school, and the mailbox is ready for use.

Mail-A-Rama

One class sponsors the "mailbox." Have the mailbox located just outside the door of that room. Children in the room become the mailmen. They deliver the blank letter forms to each classroom. Children in the school (teachers, too) write letters and mail them in this central box. At appropriate times during the day or week, the students deliver the mail.

Stamp Collections

Use blank newsprint (8½″ x 11″). Fold the desired number of sheets in half to make a book for the stamps. Use construction paper for the cover. Staple the pages and cover together at the fold. Print the name of a country on the top of each page. As children collect stamps, they can paste them on the appropriate pages. To extend this activity, children may design fantasy stamps to correspond to the real ones. Allow space in the book to add these make-believe stamps.

Interesting note: In 1840, Great Britain issued the first postage stamp. Suggest to the class that the children find out when the first stamps were issued in the United States and Canada.

Extra suggestion: To commemorate an important event at school or in the community, design a new stamp specifically to illustrate the event.

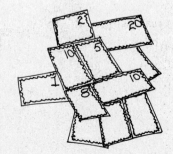

Stamp Stumpers

Ask children to bring to school collections of stamps. Large quantities of cancelled stamps may be purchased at hobby shops. Children arrange their stamps in a geometric shape on a piece of tagboard and paste them down with glue. Cover with clear shellac and allow time to dry. Use an X-acto knife or sharp scissors to cut the board into jigsaw-shaped pieces. Provide a box or large envelope to store the pieces when not in use. Provide opportunities for children to assemble each other's stamp puzzles.

Write On

Provide blank envelopes for children to practice addressing mail. Teach the correct form for addressing letters and writing the return address. Make a chart indicating the proper way to address a letter. This activity can have practical applications throughout the school year. At every opportunity, have children write letters:

1. Thank You notes to a parent or aide for assisting the class or to another class for a performance that was shared
2. Get Well cards to classmates, parents, and teachers
3. Birthday Greetings
4. Letters to authors and famous personalities expressing their feelings about their works

Extra suggestion: Watch the newspapers. Write to celebrities and political personalities to express interest, opinions, appreciation, or concern about current events.

SUGGESTED SOURCE BOOK

Keats, Ezra Jack. *A Letter to Amy.* New York: Harper and Row, 1968. Children will enjoy hearing about the special message in Peter's letter. What happens to the letter on a rainy day? After sharing the story, give children an opportunity to write special messages of their own. Let them mail the letters, but not on a rainy day!

"Mailbox" by Kevin Ancell, age 12

Stop, Look, Listen

Stop a moment
Rest a while
Take some time
To laugh and smile

Look a moment
Try to see
What nature's made
For you and me

Listen a moment
Lend an ear
So many lovely
Things to hear

STOP   LOOK   LISTEN

2

OUR FIVE SENSES

Through using their five senses children grow, develop, and learn about an exciting world around them. Activities to sharpen their awareness should be included in every primary learning program. The activities that accompany the poems in this section relate directly to the young child's learning to use his senses to find out about touching, seeing, smelling, hearing, and tasting.

When instruction on the five senses begins, have children design a "Five-Senses Folder." Suggest that they draw a hand, ear, tongue, eyes, and nose on the cover. Use this folder to collect creative writing, stories, studies, and experiments done in conjunction with the experiences presented in this section.

How Does It Feel?

Some things are soft
Like kittens I feel
Some things are hard
Like iron or steel

Some things are hot
Like fire or steam
Some things are cold
Like snow or ice cream

How Does It Feel?

STARTERS AND STRETCHERS

The hottest thing I ever touched _____.
The coldest thing I ever touched _____.
Use examples from poem "Stop, Look, Listen"
to initiate a study of antonyms—hard/soft,
fire/ice.

Have children create nonsense "feeling" words to
describe the way things feel:

"fruvelly"
"falumpy"
"blizzery"

EXTENDERS

Mr. Touch-Me

To illustrate the variety of feelings mentioned in the
poem, create a large "Mr. Touch-Me" for the classroom (see tear sheet on page 178). Have children
go on a hunt for "feeling materials" at home and
bring in samples of objects that feel different. Some
examples might include:

Mr. Touch-Me

Create texture using:
1. Varied media.
2. Line design.
3. Contrasting colors.

178

Cotton	Cork	Rubber
Foil	Burlap	Adhesive tape
Brillo pads	Sandpaper	Velvet
Metals	Sand	Wood
Silk	Plastic	Wallpaper
	Textured fabrics	

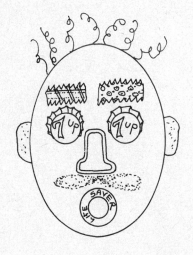

On a large sheet of paper, draw the outline of "Mr. Touch-Me" and write his name. Have children add the materials they brought from home to make his:

Hair	Eyes	Nose
Clothes	Ears	Beard
Cap	Mouth	

Include samples of materials that feel:

Hard	Waxy	Squishy
Soft	Rubbery	Scratchy
Smooth	Slick	Sticky
Rough	Bumpy	Silky
	Spongy	

After experimenting with a variety of textures, children may design their own "Mr. Touch-Me."

1. Duplicate "Mr. Touch-Me" on construction paper.
2. Children create textures by using line design (see page 73) and/or collage.
3. Children use mixed media to achieve textures: crayon resist, solid paint, pastels, markers, etc.

Mount the drawings on cardboard. Encourage children to be creative in choosing and assembling varied materials. As children complete their pictures, encourage discussion of the different materials/media used for hair, mouth, eyes, nose, and clothing.

Feeling Fingers

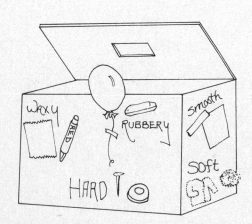

Cover a large box with butcher paper. Using a stencil and an appropriate material to illustrate how an object feels, cut out the following words and glue them on the box:

Smooth	(fabric, paper, plastic)
Hard	(marbles, checkers, Lifesavers)
Soft	(cotton balls, velvet)
Waxy	(wax paper)
Rubbery	(flat rubber sponge, cut rubber bands)

Ask children to bring in assorted materials for the box. Cut an opening in the top. Children will enjoy reaching into the box, feeling the objects, and describing how they felt.

Touch and Guess. Each child takes a turn reaching into the box, feeling the object, and guessing what it is. Then he pulls the object out to see if he has guessed correctly.

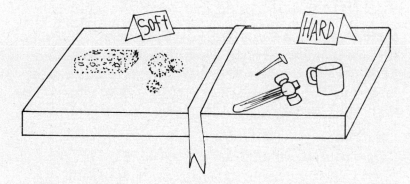

Touch and Sort. Place all the feeling objects on a table. The child will classify the objects according to the following properties:

Hard/Soft
Smooth/Rough
Thick/Thin

The child may choose more than two items and put them in order: from soft to hard, smooth to rough, cold to warm, etc.

Chart Racks

Begin small charts with titles:

Things Feel Soft
Things Feel Hard
Things Feel Rough
Things Feel Smooth

Have children cut pictures out of magazines to illustrate various feelings. Glue the pictures to the chart and label the item by name. *Variation:* Glue appropriate actual materials to the chart.

Helping Hands

Blindfold one child at a time. Lead him to a spot in the classroom and see if he can guess the location by touching. Have children try to identify various classroom objects while blindfolded.

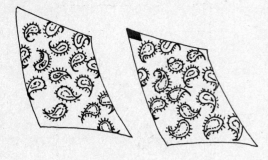

Match-Up or Concentration

Cut textured fabrics or wallpaper samples into three-inch squares. Cut two identical squares of each fabric. Mount each square on a separate index card. Mark a dark corner on one of each fabric pair.

Match-up. Place cards with dark corners face up on a table. Divide the unmarked cards into two equal piles. Divide the class into two teams, giving each team one pile of cards. Each child takes a turn. The first team to match all of the cards with their duplicates is the winning team.

Concentration. The cards are shuffled. A player turns over two cards. If he draws a matching pair, he may keep them; if not, he must discard one card face down on the table. The next player repeats the process. The player with the greatest number of matching pairs wins.

Texturize: Feeling Collages

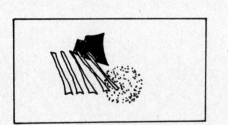

Give each child a piece of tagboard or cardboard cut to a manageable size. Gather materials of many textures. Arrange them on the board and glue them in place to form a desired shape or design. Some suggestions of varied paper textures to use:

Tissue   Sandpaper
Construction   Textured wallpaper
Newspaper

Textured Autographs

Children can write their names in many textures. On a piece of cardboard, the child writes his name in glue and sprinkles sand over the entire area. Allow time to dry; shake off excess sand. The same procedure can be repeated using tiny pebbles, pieces of cotton, glitter, cornmeal, or cereal.

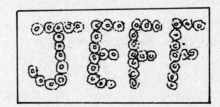

Thumb Fun

Have the child press his thumb on an ink pad. Then have him "print" with it on white paper. Discover what kinds of animals and people can be created. For variety, print with fingers, too. Use fine-line markers to add detail to the designs.

Fantasy Hands

Have children trace their hands with a pencil or crayon on a large sheet of paper. Give the following directions slowly: "Keep turning the paper. Keep tracing. Trace two fingers. Trace one finger. STOP!

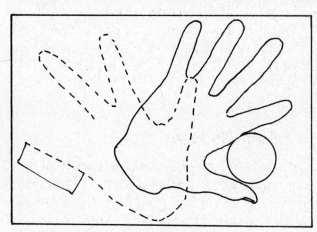

Do you see an animal, person, or object? Add some geometric shapes. STOP! Now what do you see? Use colors, lines, and designs to decorate your picture."

The Hands of an Artist

Let children experiment by touching and feeling works in different media of many artists. Let their fingers examine all kinds of sculpture, weavings, tapestries, mosaics, and paintings.

Textured Paint

Experiment with many brush strokes and varied amounts of paint. How can different textures be achieved?

SUGGESTED SOURCE BOOKS

Podendorf, Illa. *Touching for Telling.* Chicago: Children's Press (Regensteiner Publishing), 1971. Illustrated by Florence Frederick. This book presents a wide range of learning discoveries possible through the sense of touch, including numerous experiments of things to do. Explanations are included for using fingers to feel, see, and hear.

Showers, Paul. *Find Out by Touching.* New York: Thomas Y. Crowell, 1961. Illustrated by Robert Galster. An understanding of the importance of the sense of touch is developed by presenting a simple and cleverly illustrated game for children to play. Children do not always have to see in order to identify an object. Children are exposed to items that are soft, hard, smooth, rough, sharp, warm, and cold. An appreciation for the sense of touch is quickly developed.

"How Does It Feel?" by Angela Selesnick, age 3½

"How Does It Feel?" by Eric Feigenbaum, age 6

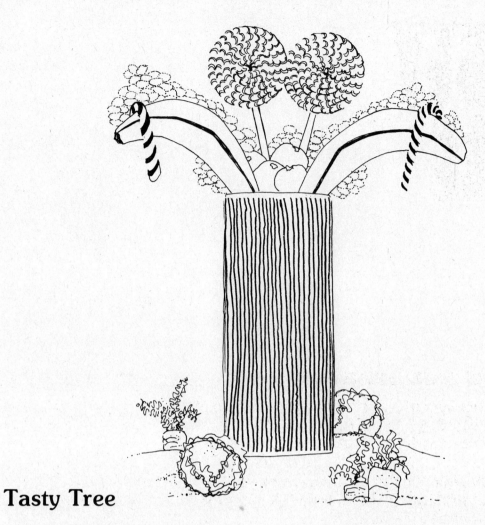

Tasty Tree

I saw the most fantastic tree
The bark of chocolate bars
The branches made of sugarcane
Instead of leaves grew jars

> Of candy canes
> And lemon drops
> Salty nuts
> And lollipops
> Bubble gum
> And marshmallows
> Spicy cakes
> And jelly rolls

On other branches hung some food
All scrumptious and delicious
Many fruits and vegetables
So healthy and nutritious

> String beans
> And tomatoes
> Asparagus
> Potatoes
> Bananas
> Pears and cherries
> Grapefruits
> And blueberries

Instead of grass and flowers
Were carrot sprouts to see
Cabbages and lettuce
Around the Tasty Tree

TASTY TREE

STARTERS AND STRETCHERS

Have children compile a list of their favorite foods. Rewrite "Tasty Tree" to include the children's favorite foods and eliminate those foods they do not like.

Have each child choose a country. Rewrite the poem by substituting foods from that country for foods mentioned in the poem.

Food Fantasies: If I were the cook in my house. . . . If I were lost in the forest I would survive by. . . . If I could open a restaurant. . . .

EXTENDERS

Build a Tasty Tree

Use a large branch from a tree. Sink the end into a heavy ball of clay. Spray the tree any color (pink or purple would be delicious). Decide on different ways things taste:

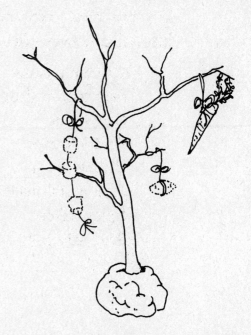

Sweet	(gumdrops, marshmallows, lollipops)
Sour	(lemons)
Salty	(potato chips, pretzels)
Bitter	(instant coffee granules, radishes)
Spicy	(flavored taco chips, dry mustard, pepper)
Crunchy	(raw vegetables, peanuts, popcorn)

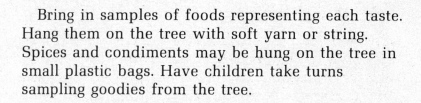

Bring in samples of foods representing each taste. Hang them on the tree with soft yarn or string. Spices and condiments may be hung on the tree in small plastic bags. Have children take turns sampling goodies from the tree.

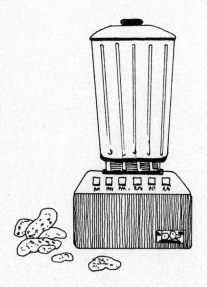

From Peanuts to Peanut Butter

Have children shell and sample fresh peanuts and describe the taste. Put two cups of shelled, fresh-roasted peanuts in a blender. Blend until chunky. Add some salt if desired. What happened to the peanuts? Does the taste change? Describe the change in terms of texture, taste, smell, and quantity.

Peanut Butter Happy-Face Snack Treats

Ingredients needed:

> Peanut butter
> Round crackers
> Raisins
> Plastic spreader

Children spread the peanut butter on the crackers. They use raisins to make eyes and a happy smile. How does it taste?

Taste Changes

What foods taste and look different when they are raw and when they are cooked? Experiment with slices of fresh apple. Try making baked apples in a toaster oven. Then try apple sauce. Did the cooking affect the taste?

A Tasting Party

Have a "Tasting Party" at school. Each child brings in one food (or spice or condiment) to be sampled. Children take turns being blindfolded and guessing what they taste. The same game can be played using fruit-flavored Lifesavers and having the children guess the flavor.

International Tasting

Give children opportunities to taste foods of other countries. Using a toaster oven, an electric skillet, and a hot plate, many foods may be easily prepared in a classroom. Some exotic suggestions might include:

Mexico: tacos, tostadas, enchiladas
Italy: spaghetti, individual pizzas made by spreading tomato sauce, cheese, and oregano on English muffins
Japan: raw vegetables stir-fried in a little oil in an electric skillet
Hawaii: tropical fruit drinks with lots of pineapple, coconut, and cherry juices

Food for Thought

Introduce the concept of the importance of proper eating habits and a balanced diet. Present the four basic food groups:

Protein   Fruits and Vegetables
Carbohydrates   Dairy Products

Examine the foods mentioned in the poem and classify them according to the basic food groups.

People Plates

To emphasize the importance of good eating habits, design "People Plates." Use brightly colored paper plates. Collect all kinds of cereal:

Corn Flakes   Cheerios
Bran   Shredded Wheat

Glue cereal to the plate to form eyes, nose, mouth, and hair. Bulletin board caption: "You Are What You Eat."

Menu Mania

Collect as many menus as you can from local restaurants. Create a center where children can "order" their foods. Choose waiters and waitresses to take the orders, tally the cost, and "serve" the food. Which restaurant is the most popular? Why?

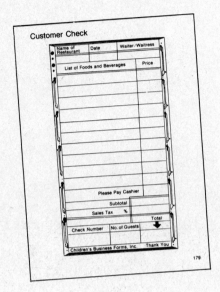

Restaurant Business

When children have had sufficient opportunity to examine the menus, they will be ready to open their own restaurants. This activity can be a research project to present simple economic concepts. Or, children can create their own restaurants using their imaginations.

Have children choose a name for the restaurant and identify the type of food it will serve. Each child creates an appropriate logo (an identifying design or symbol). Children design the menus, listing the types of foods and beverages available and the corresponding prices. Have children exchange finished menus and "order" selections of their choosing. Use the "Customer Check" tear sheet on page 179 to write orders and prices. When orders are complete, have children add up the total cost of the bill. Add the sales tax. The totals may be checked on an adding machine.

This activity could be extended to include establishing individual restaurants in the classroom and using play money to pay the bill. Children can find out which restaurant does the best business and discuss why.

Take a Taste Survey

Each child chooses four of his favorite foods and writes them on "My Survey" tear sheet (page 172). Child interviews his friends to discover which foods they like best. Choices are recorded on the survey sheet and transferred to the "My Graph" tear sheet (page 173). Conclusions are drawn from the information gathered and reported on "My Findings" tear sheet (page 174). See pages 129–30 for specific instructions.

Tongue Zones

Design a "Tasty Treat Game Board." Cut out a giant tongue from tagboard. On the game board identify the parts of the tongue that receive the following sensations:

Sweet   Salty
Bitter   Sour

Small pictures of foods are cut out and mounted individually on file cards. Players take turns drawing a card and attaching it to the proper area of the tongue.

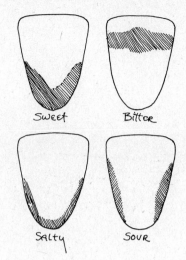

Tasty Colors

How does color relate to taste? Use crayons, pastels, or paint to show primary and secondary colors. Show foods related to these colors. Examples might include:

Red: apple, tomato
Yellow: banana, lemon
Orange: orange, tangerine
Green: lettuce, cucumber
Purple: plum, eggplant

See how many foods can be associated with a color.

Design Individual Tasty Tree

Use the "Tasty Tree" tear sheet on page 180. Duplicate the tree on construction paper. Using drawings, magazine pictures of foods, or actual foods, create a collage on the tree. The finished tree may be mounted inside a box lid to create a shadowbox effect. The frame of the box may be decorated with the child's favorite food.

Many opportunities exist to use the "Tasty Tree":

1. Fill the tree with "sensible snacks."
2. Fill the tree with the foods you love. Be sure to include some foods from each of the basic food groups.
3. Fill the tree with small drawings of everything the child ate in one day. How many of the foods were healthy? How many were tasty? How many were healthy and tasty?

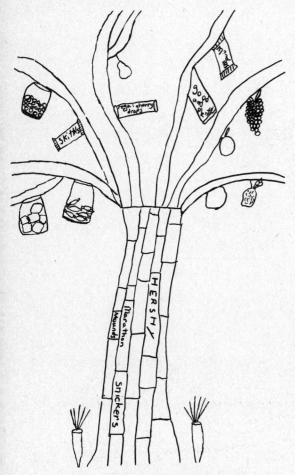

"Tasty Tree" by Kate Wilson, age 11

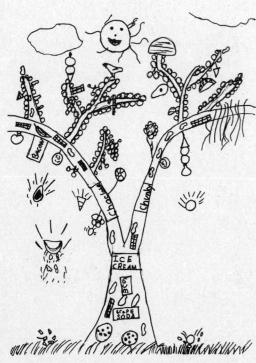

"Tasty Tree" by Jessica Day, age 9

Tasty Tree for Zoo or Barnyard Animals

Select an animal and draw it in the corner of the "Tasty Tree" tear sheet (page 180). Several animals might be represented on one tree. Some suggested taste treats for animals:

Monkeys: bananas
Frogs, Toads: insects
Horses, Cows: hay
Rabbits, Guinea Pigs: carrots
Squirrels: acorns
Elephants: peanuts
Birds: worms
Bears: honey

SUGGESTED SOURCE BOOKS

Hoban, Russell. *Bread and Jam for Frances.* New York: Harper and Row, 1964. Illustrated by Lillian Hoban.

Read the story and share the illustrations with the class.

Why did Frances prefer bread and jam?
Why did Frances begin to feel "full of jam"?
Have you ever felt like Frances?

Imagine that Frances is coming to dinner. Plan a menu that you think she would enjoy. Use a paper plate. Draw or cut out pictures of food and fill the plate with dinner for Frances. Explain why you chose each food.

Slepian, Jan, and Seidler, Ann. *The Hungry Thing.* Chicago: Follett, 1967. Illustrated by Richard E. Martin. Children will enjoy meeting The Hungry Thing with an insatiable appetite for nonsense foods. High on its favorite-food list are "shmancakes," "tickles," "feetloaf," and "hookies." The townspeople are quite perplexed about the demands of The Hungry Thing. Finally they interpret his message and The Hungry Thing is most appreciative. After reading the book, give children an opportunity to dramatize the story. Choose one child to be The Hungry Thing, while the rest of the children act as the townspeople, creating new and imaginative foods to feed this hungry creature. Foods may be drawn, labelled, cut out of colored paper, and pasted on paper plates. Simple costumes may be used.

64

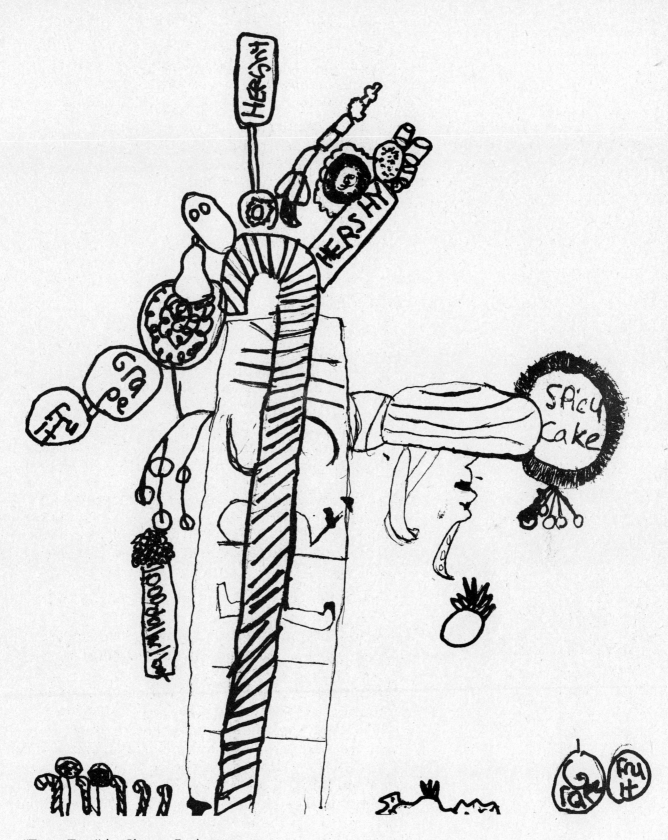

"Tasty Tree" by Sharon Burke, age 11

65

Stuffy Nose

I have a cold, my nose is stuffed
I cannot smell a thing
I cannot smell the flowers that
My friend came by to bring

I cannot smell the turkey that
My mom put in to bake
I cannot smell the cinnamon
And spices on the cake

I have a cold, my nose is stuffed
I just want to get well.
What if I forget and don't
Remember how to smell?

Stuffy Nose

STARTERS AND STRETCHERS

Define *palate:* A pleasurable taste sensation (also, the roof of the mouth). Define *palette:* A board used by painters to mix colors.

What if I forgot how to smell? How would my life be affected? Would other senses compensate for my loss?

Experiment to find out how taste is related to smell. Blindfold one child and have him hold his nose while he tastes. Give him samples of cut-up raw fruits and vegetables. Could the child distinguish among them? While the child is chewing, have him stop holding his nose. Now he will be able to identify the food.

EXTENDERS

Design a Smell Box for the Classroom

Use empty medicine vials available from a pharmacist. Fill each one with a different-smelling substance. Some examples might include:

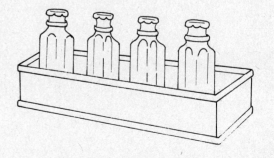

Coffee	Iodine	Mouthwash
Onion	Lemon	Rubbing alcohol
Dill	Cinnamon	Eau de cologne
Pepper	Flower petals	Soap

You might also include extracts of peppermint, banana, coconut, and vanilla.

Cover the vials with masking tape so that the contents will remain a mystery. Place the vials in a small box with a number on top of each vial. Provide paper and the opportunity for each child to record his guess of the contents. When all the children have had a chance to smell, reveal the correct answers.

Smell Safari

Describe the smells in the poem "Stuffy Nose." Are they pleasant? Have children go on a "Smell Safari" at home or in the school cafeteria. Decide which smells are most pleasant and discuss why.

Smells for All Seasons

Describe the types of smells that you would notice:

1. On an icy winter morning (roasting chestnuts)
2. On a crisp fall afternoon (leaves crackling in a fireplace)
3. On a hot, humid summer day (waterfalls, creeks, and foliage in the countryside)
4. On a beautiful spring morning (freshly cut grass and flowers beginning to bloom)

Nose Aids

Ask children if they have ever noticed food that turned sour or rancid. How does the sense of smell help determine whether the food is still edible? Have children use their sense of smell to decide whether all the foods in their refrigerator are fresh. (Adult supervision is recommended.)

Art Scents

Discover the odors of art media:

Oil pastels	Clay	Stone
Chalk	Wood	Metal
Crayon	Plaster	Paper
Pencils	Linseed oil	Plasticine
Marking pens	Tape	Leather
Ink pens	Plastic	Paints (poster, oil, acrylic, finger paints)

In art, these odors comprise the "odor palette."

Color Scents

How does color relate to odor? Give the following directions to children: "Close your eyes. Think of one color. How does it smell? How many things can you think of that smell that color?"

Use the "Odor Palette" tear sheet on page 181. Children find magazine pictures, drawings, or use actual items that typify the "smell" of each color. Examples:

1. Food smells
2. Objects in nature
3. Types of art materials

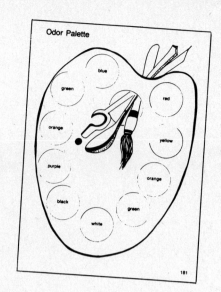

On the "Odor Palette," *food smells* are represented by the spoon; *art media odors* are represented by the paintbrush; *miscellaneous odors* of all types are represented by the question mark (things found in nature: grass, flowers, animal scents). Completed palettes may be mounted on cardboard to be shared with others.

SUGGESTED SOURCE BOOKS

Aliki (pseud.). *My Five Senses.* New York: Thomas Y. Crowell, 1962. The book presents a greater appreciation and understanding of discovery through the five senses. Clever illustrations vividly describe each of the senses.

Bendick, Jeanne. *The Human Senses.* New York: Franklin Watts, 1968. Illustrated by Jeanne Bendick. The book presents a scientific explanation of the five senses, discussing inner senses, reflexes, memory, life experiences, and making inferences as they relate to sense perception. Many fun learning experiments are included.

Showers, Paul. *Follow Your Nose.* New York: Thomas Y. Crowell, 1963. Illustrated by Paul Galdone. A wonderful book of science information about the sense of smell. The book includes easy experiments that demonstrate the relationship of smell to taste. The functions of the nose are presented with delightful accompanying illustrations.

"Stuffy Nose" by Lori Fox, age 8

Magnifying Glass

Through a magnifying glass
Things are large and clear
When looking very closely
Amazing things appear

A great rainbow of colors
In the sky or on the ground
Tones and hues all blending
New colors to be found

A million different shapes
On a tree of oak or pine
Lines and textures mixing
To create a new design

So if you really want to look
The whole world magnifies
And you don't need a special glass
Just learn to use your eyes!

MAGNIFYING GLASS

STARTERS AND STRETCHERS

In conjunction with developing the sense of sight, work to build and extend visual imagery in children. After the first reading of "Magnifying Glass," ask the children to close their eyes and read it to them again. Ask them about the "rainbow" image in the poem.

> How long is it?
> How many colors are there in it?
> How high does it reach?
> Can you capture it? How?
> Where is the "oak tree"?
> What shape are its branches?
> How old is it?
> How tall does it stand?

EXTENDERS

Nature Walks

Give children plenty of opportunity to observe objects in nature firsthand. Give children clipboards to record their observations as they walk. Encourage them to pay attention to detail.

71

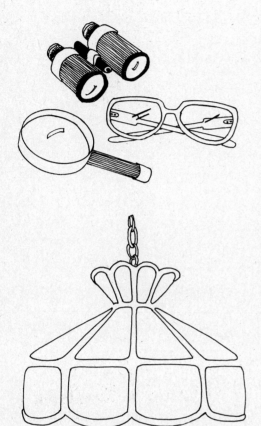

Memory Eyes

Place fifteen familiar objects on a tray. Have children study them for a minute. Remove the tray of objects and see how many the children can recall. Ask which sense helps them to remember.

Optic Aid

Start a collection of instruments, utensils, and objects that are aids in seeing. Include a magnifying glass, microscope, binoculars, sunglasses, mirror, pane of window glass, telescope. Teach children the function of each. Look at small objects through each of these optical devices and discuss the special effects of each.

Focus In

Looking and really seeing any object is the most important lesson to learn in the process of creating art images. Show any large object that has many shapes, lines, and designs. Point out the object's geometric shapes, contour lines, and design lines.

Shadows and Reflections

How are they alike?
How are they different?
How can each be created?

The Shadow Game. Have one child be an image—an animal, a person, etc. Choose another child to be the shadow of that image. Have the class decide whether the shadow can keep up with the image. The same game can be played by having one child be another child's reflection.

Draw a Shadow. Place a bicycle outside so that it casts a shadow that the children can see. Give each child a large sheet of paper, a pencil, and an eraser. Children draw the shadow of the bike: the outside (exterior) and inside (interior) contour lines. Include spokes, wheels, seat, etc. Children bring their finished contour drawings into the room and add color and design.

Eye Exchange

Imagine the world through the eyes of others.
Examples:

> How does the world look to a butterfly? To a monkey in the zoo?
>
> To a giraffe? To an ant? To a beetle?
>
> How does our classroom look to Jeff's baby sister?
>
> To a younger child? To an older child?

Contour Drawing

Set up a still life of flowers and leaves. Have children draw what they see without looking at their paper. Suggest that they draw slowly: "The pencil is like an ant crawling across a page." At certain points the children may look at their papers. Stress individual creativity, *not* realism. When the children have practiced contour drawing, give them black paper (for contrast) and chalk or oil pastels. They can create their own flower still life.

Line Design

Discuss the properties of lines with children. Lines don't have to be straight. They can be curved, zig-zag, or broken. Show examples of each. After children have had a chance to experiment with lines, have them create their own designs. Use the "Decorate the Room" tear sheet on page 182. Children use line design to upholster the chair, weave the carpet, ornament the lamp, and create an abstract painting.

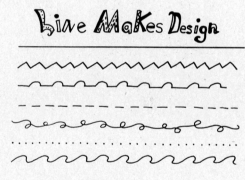

Geometric Drawing

Children experiment by drawing geometric shapes on paper. The shapes may overlap. Draw a triangle, circle, square, cylinder, rectangle, oval, and diamond. Ask the children to put the shapes together to make a person. Make him move by changing the position of the shapes. See the "Geometric Man" tear sheet on page 183 as an example.

1. Duplicate the "Geometric Man" on colored paper.
2. Make a list of the shapes on the "Geometric Man" (circle, oval, rectangle, triangle, cylinder, prism, and arc).
3. Write the "shape" words on the shapes that they identify.

Extra suggestion: Decorate the "Geometric Man" using both line design and solid color.

Vocabulary Building: Art Talk

Geometric Drawing
Contour Drawing
Gesture Drawing
Line Design
Thumbnail Sketch
Positive and Negative Space
Collage
Sculpture
Media
Abstract Painting
Realistic Painting
Impressionistic Painting
Pointillism

SUGGESTED SOURCE BOOKS

Anderson, Hans Christian. *The Emperor's New Clothes.* New York: Random House, 1971. Children will enjoy this classic story about the emperor whose sense of sight told him one thing while his sense of pride told him another.

Emberley, Ed. *Make a World*. Boston: Little, Brown, 1972. Everyday objects are formed by beginning a drawing with a simple geometric shape. A step-by-step progression for each drawing is shown.

_____. *Drawing Book of Animals*. Boston: Little, Brown, 1970. A step-by-step progression is used to draw members of the animal kingdom. These books are excellent learning center materials.

MacAgy, Douglas, and MacAgy, Elizabeth. *Going for a Walk with a Line*. Garden City, N.Y.: Doubleday, 1959. Introduction written by Vincent Price. The book describes the fascinating directions a line may travel as seen in the works of these modern artists: Edgar Degas, Marc Chagall, Joan Miró, Piet Mondrian, Pablo Picasso, and Salvador Dali.

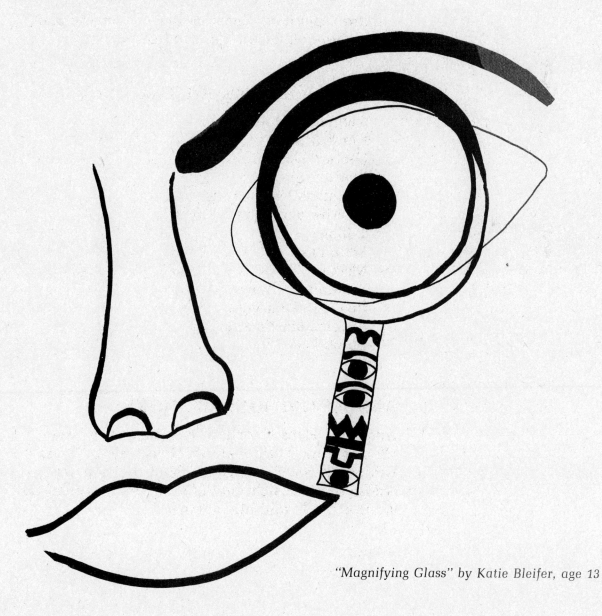

"Magnifying Glass" by Katie Bleifer, age 13

Hearing Aid

I have a special hearing aid
That I tune in or out
It can plug into a whisper
It can register a shout

I can turn it off completely
And make things very quiet
It blocks out all the noises
Oh, you should really try it

Now sometimes it gets broken
On any kind of day
And I might miss important things
That people have to say

But I can learn to fix it
If I decide to hear
Because my special hearing aid
Is really my own Ear

Hearing Aid

STARTERS AND STRETCHERS

The loudest noise I ever heard: _____.
The most important words I ever heard:
_____.
The best news I ever heard: _____.

EXTENDERS

Sound Survey

Have children take a "sound survey" on the way to school. Ask them to describe some of the sounds they heard. Make a list of these sounds and try to re-create them in the classroom.

Classroom Clatter

Have children close their eyes and identify familiar sounds in the classroom:

A clock ticking
A chair being pushed
A book being dropped
Footsteps
Chalk writing on the chalkboard

Sounds help create visual images in our minds. Have children cut out pictures from magazines of objects that create sounds. Classify the pictures in various categories:

Home sounds/School sounds
Inside sounds/Outside sounds
Soft sounds/Loud sounds

Barnyard Noises

Talk about the sounds animals make. Have children use rhythm instruments and voices to reproduce these sounds. Record them on a tape recorder. Play them back and ask others to guess what animals make these sounds.

Put On a Sound Show

Have children create sounds that are funny, scary, happy, spooky, jolly, and pretty. Draw a picture to go with each sound. Use the "Make a Melody" tear sheet on page 184. Children use voices, rhythm instruments, parts of their bodies, and objects in the room.

Have children invent sounds that are loud, soft, smooth, hard, squeaky, high, low, fast, and slow. Ask children to give a solo performance or to join with other children to form an "orchestra." Each "player" will have his own interpretation of each sound.

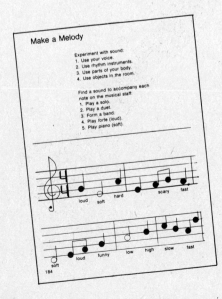

Patterns of Sound

Have children experiment with patterns. (A pattern is something that repeats itself.) Experiment with color and shape. Have children cut out many small geometric shapes of assorted colors. Paste them on paper to form a pattern. Assign a sound for each shape:

○ = clap
△ = boom
□ = shhh!

Now play your melody.

Vocabulary Building: Musical Talk

Use a music text or a music specialist as a resource. Help children develop an understanding of the following musical terms:

Treble clef
Bass clef
Musical staff
Signature
Whole note, Whole rest
Half note, Half rest
Quarter note, Quarter rest
Piano
Forte

Design a Sound Band

Children use bells, foil, wood, cans, or paper cups to construct their own instruments for the sound band. Define all kinds of music:

Jazz
Rock
Classical
Popular
Country-Western

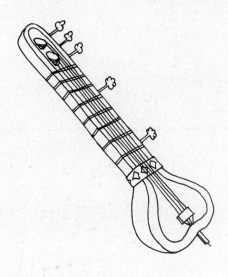

Encourage children to use their imagination to create instruments from varied materials that produce unique sounds. When instruments are completed, "strike up the band" for all to enjoy!

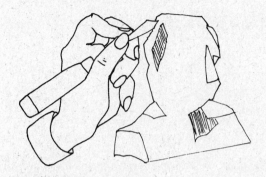

Sounds of Art

Have children experiment to discover the sounds associated with the following processes:

1. Varied amounts of pressure applied to a pencil when drawing
2. A variety of strokes in painting—for example, little dots painted fast (pointillism)
3. Washes—using a paintbrush and watercolors to create a wash over a surface of paper
4. The different sounds of sculpture:
   Pounding clay as compared to molding clay
   Welding a sculpture
   Pouring liquid plaster
   Sanding a surface smooth

Listen and Paint

Several children can work together on a large sheet of paper or mural while music is playing. How did the tempo of the music determine the strokes represented?

SUGGESTED SOURCE BOOK

McGovern, Ann. *Too Much Noise.* Boston: Houghton-Mifflin, 1967. Children will enjoy reading about Peter and his troubles with his old, old house. One by one, sounds are first added and then eliminated. Children will be able to relate to the effects of noise pollution.

"Hearing Aid" by Jill Donnerstag, age 6

"Hearing Aid" by Kari Katzman, age 6

I Hear a Smile

The rhythm of two skipping feet
The lively shout to those you meet

The hands that clap so happily
The whistle of a melody

If I listen for a while
I can really hear a smile

3
ME
AND MY
FEELINGS

Teachers and parents share the responsibility of helping the child build a strong, healthy self-concept. A child who has a good feeling about himself is successful in his everyday interactions with peers and adults. Emphasizing a trusting relationship and open communication between students and their parents and teachers helps ensure that the child will develop a good self-image, which can affect future learning.

The poems and learning experiences in this section focus on the child and his feelings. They encourage the child to conceptualize the feelings expressed in the poems in order to motivate a greater self-awareness—which forms the basis for self-esteem. This section creates an environmental setting for "hearing" our feelings.

Please note, however, that although the teacher may encourage open communication of thoughts and emotions, if a child does not wish to share his feelings, he always has the option of keeping them private.

Some of the poems in this section are presented exclusive of accompanying activities. This creates an opportunity to develop poetry appreciation for its own sake. Reading poetry helps children relate to the experiences of others. (Some suggestions about reading poetry were presented in the Introduction to this book.) *Reading* poetry may naturally stimulate the child to write original poems. *Writing* poetry can vividly sharpen the child's awareness of his own experiences.

Imagine That!

I walked up to my house one day
And opened up the door
The floor was on the ceiling
The ceiling on the floor

I went to get an ice cream
And climbed upon a chair
And right inside the freezer
There sat a polar bear

I looked outside my window
And saw my friend fly by
Orange juice and lemonade
Were raining from the sky

I opened up my closet
And watched my shoes and hat
March right out to meet me
Can you imagine that!

IMAGINE THAT!

STARTERS AND STRETCHERS

Clear the floor
Stack the shelves
Fill the drawers
Change ourselves
   into buyers, manufacturers, and salespeople
Customers will crowd the door
We're opening a children's store!

EXTENDERS

Imagine That, Inc.: A Children's Store

Hire a staff:

1. Owner-Manager.
2. Sales Manager: Supervises
salespeople, hires salespeople,
and reports to owner.

ORGANIZATIONAL CHART

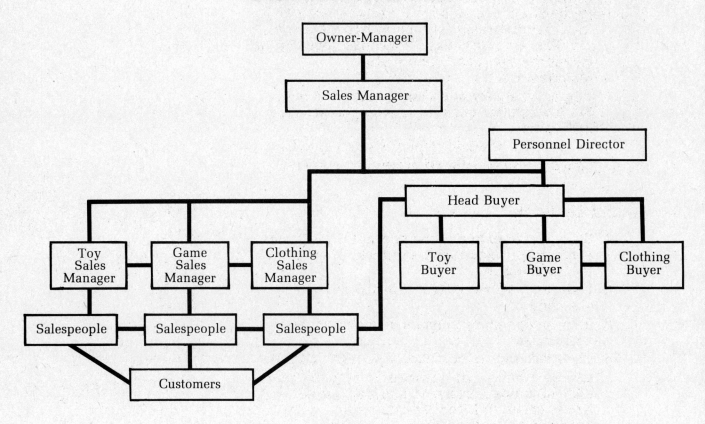

3. Salesperson: Sells items to customers.
4. Personnel Director: Hires salespeople and determines their salary by conferring with Sales Manager. Salespeople are paid either a base salary or a ten-percent commission on their sales.
5. Head Buyer: Responsible for hiring and supervising toy buyer and clothes buyer. The Head Buyer consults with the Personnel Director to determine the salary for buyers and finds out from salespeople which items are selling. He or she then tells the buyers how much they can spend on new items for the store.

Store Starters

Organizing a store in the classroom may be done in many ways.

1. Children may bring in actual items that they wish to sell. (Permission from home suggested.)
2. Children may find pictures of items in toy catalogues. These may be cut out and mounted in a bulletin board "store window."

3. Children may produce their own items to sell in the store—for example, puppets, wooden toys, painted rocks, stitchery, batik T-shirts, etc. Those children who make the toys can be called the toy, game, and clothes manufacturers.

4. The Head Buyer and associate buyers mark the prices after consulting with the producer of the item.

5. A specified amount of play money may be issued to each child when the store opens.

Grand Opening

1. Salespeople organize merchandise. They may need to add new items, or stock. They unlock the cash register.

2. Customer walks in. He wants to buy a skateboard.

3. Salesperson shows customer different types and prices.

4. Customer buys a skateboard for $10 in cash.

5. Use the "Sales Slip" tear sheet on page 185. List the items purchased and their prices. Salesperson will total the sales slip. Salesperson may write the sales slip in duplicate. One copy is given to the customer. This is a receipt. ("Sales Slip" may be used as a general classroom math activity.)

6. At the end of the day, the salesperson adds the total sales from the duplicate sales slips and reports to the Sales Manager.

7. The Owner-Manager deposits the money in the bank.

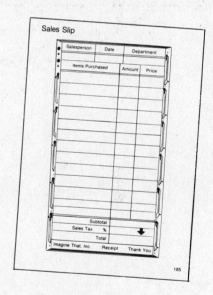

Extra suggestion: Some customers may buy an item and write a check or use a charge account to pay for it. Children can research this.

Vocabulary Building: Shop Talk

Inventory (stock)
Producer (goods and services)
Consumer
Product
Resources
Profit and Loss
Income
Investment
Manufacturer

"Imagine That!"
  by Stacey Tuchin, age 5½

"Imagine That!"
  by Feoktist Orloff, age 6

"Imagine That!"
  by Helaine Thau, age 9

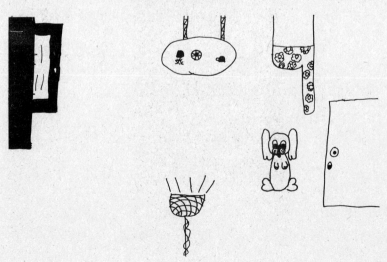

"Imagine That!" by Michael Bell, age 9

Faces

I painted a face
That was angry
I painted the mouth
In a frown

I painted a face
That was puzzled
I painted the head
Upside down

I painted a face
That was curious
I painted the eyes
Large and bright

I painted a face
That was sad
I painted it all
Dark as night

I painted a face
That was proud
I painted the chin
Straight and high

I painted a face
That was happy
I painted a gleam
In the eye

FACES

STARTERS AND STRETCHERS

Children count the faces described in the poem. Have children use a mirror to imitate the expressions represented. Draw a face to show each feeling. Can you think of other feelings that our faces show?

EXTENDERS

People Pots

Either clay or dough may be used effectively as the medium.

Clay: Use a rolling pin to flatten clay to one-half inch thickness. Using a large, empty juice can, cut out two circles of clay. One circle is the base of the pot. The other will be used as the lid. Give children a small ball of clay and ask each child to roll out four "snakes" (coils) of clay. Attach the coils one at a time to the base, forming a coil pot. Form the lid by attaching a small ball of clay to the other circle. Pinch and pull it to create a face. Paint the clay and arrange to have it fired in a kiln, if possible. Apply clear shellac after firing for a shiny finish.

Dough: See recipe for making dough on page 26. Follow the procedure described above for making the pot and the lid. Bake the unpainted pot and lid in a 350° oven for about one hour. Allow time to cool, and color with markers. Spray with clear shellac.

Face File

Have children find pictures in magazines to illustrate different feelings. Mount each face on 8½" x 11" construction paper. Children will decide what feeling is described by the face and label their picture. Using heavy dividers, make a file and sort the faces by feeling categories.

Use the "Face File" for Creative Writing. Select a picture from the file for creative writing. Describe the feelings of the face in the picture. What is it about the face that expresses this emotion? Has your face ever looked like this?

Design a Patchwork Quilt of Many Faces

Provide colored construction paper squares (6" x 6"). Have children use markers to draw a face representing a feeling they have had:

Happy	Frustrated
Sad	Pain
Good	Love
Alone	Special
Jealous	

Label the picture with its appropriate feeling word. Pin all of the faces side by side on a large bulletin board. Use heavy yarn, rickrack, or colored paper strips to outline each square of the quilt. Finishing touch: Add lace or eyelet for border.

Tower of Feelings

Children make lists of words to describe feelings. Each child designs a "Tower of Feelings" by writing each word in different-colored marking pens on a sheet of art paper. Arrange the words on the paper in the shape of a tower. Towers can be shared and discussed.

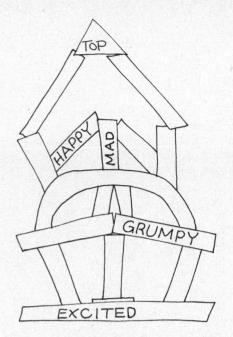

Ladder of Feelings

Design a ladder with seven or eight rungs. Print a feeling word on each rung. Have the children "climb" the ladders, read the feelings, and tell when that feeling occurred.

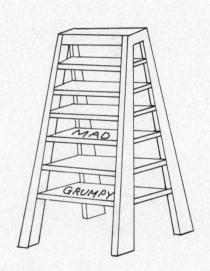

Mirror Image

Read the poem "Faces" and ask children to listen carefully and try to relate to a specific feeling. Use the "Mirror Image" tear sheet on page 186.

1. Ask the children how they feel. Have them draw their feeling on a face in the mirror on the tear sheet.
2. Use line design to decorate the border of the mirror.
3. Use *one* word to describe the face on the "Telltale Tag."

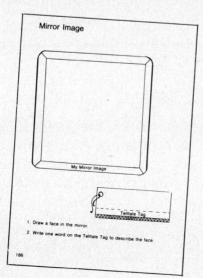

93

Mirror Image Game ("Tag-It"). Children cut out their mirrors and "Telltale Tags." Display the mirrors. Put the tags in a box. Children choose a tag and place it on the image described by the tag.

A Reflection of Me

Children attach a small pocket mirror inside the lid of a shoe box. Suggest that they decorate the inside of the lid with symbols that reflect their interests and personalities. Encourage individuality of expression. Some suggestions might include:

> A thumb print (each child's is different)
> Pictures brought from home
> Cut out magazine pictures of foods, sports, and hobbies that interest the child.

When the inside of the lid is completely decorated, wrap the outside edges with heavy yarn, using glue to hold the yarn in place. Attach a large loop of yarn at one end to hang the lid.

A Gallery of Faces

Faces can show:

> Personality
> Occupation
> Age
> Nationality
> Health

Design a collage from cut-out magazine photographs that reflect the above qualities. Children may wish to make a collage of their own family pictures.

Extra suggestion: Photographic negatives may be used for the collage.

"Faces" by Tara Stephenson, age 6

Mask Making

In ancient times, masks were used for rituals, dances, or display. Masks reflected happiness, sadness, or fear and were often used as protection from evil spirits. Masks were made from wood, copper, and clay. Three-dimensional features of the mask were painted, designed, and exaggerated.

Sometimes the mask covered the entire body. When a person put on the mask, he began to assume the emotion reflected in the features.*

Uses of masks today:

1. To entertain people
2. To look and feel different (for example, Halloween costumes)
3. Makeup (to look better)

SUGGESTED SOURCE BOOKS

Berger, Terry. *I Have Feelings.* New York: Behavioral Press, 1971. After reading the story to the children, ask them to identify the many feelings that were expressed. Give them a large sheet of art paper, colored chalk, and lots of encouragement to draw one of their feelings. In a private conference, ask the child to identify the feeling and find out why it occurred. Help children understand that feelings exist in everyone. As children learn to express their feelings, they can learn to deal with them.

Saroyan, William. *Me.* New York: Crowell Collier Press, 1963. Children will enjoy the text and illustrations of this delightful book depicting a world with one word, "ME."

Design a "ME" folder. Use dark crayons to write "ME" many times on a large sheet of art paper. Tracing letters may be used effectively. Use a watercolor wash to cover the paper. This can be used as a folder for stories and poems written for and about "ME."

*Reference: H. W. Janson, *History of Art* (Englewood Cliffs, N.J.: Prentice-Hall, 1965).

"Faces" by Jon Katzman, age 9

Growing Pains

As I'm growing up I know
Different feelings start to show

Sometimes when I'm happy
I want to laugh and shout
Sometimes when I'm lonely
I want to mope and pout

Sometimes when I'm angry
I want to cry and scream
Sometimes when I'm all alone
I want to sit and dream

growing pains

STARTERS AND STRETCHERS

Job Hunting. Children make a list and research specific occupations. Each child writes a story, "I would like to be a _____."

Occupational Hazards. Children research and write the difficulties or hazards of their chosen occupation.

EXTENDERS

Life Cycles

Have children design stepping-stones to represent significant landmarks in their growth and development. Have them use one stepping-stone to represent each event. Use the "Stepping-Stones" tear sheet on page 187. Have children project the future by adding stepping-stones to represent life events as they predict them. Pictures and/or sentences may be used. The arrows provide space for elaboration.

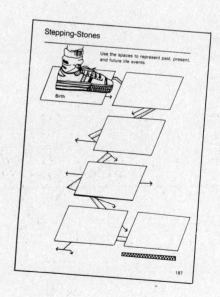

Time Lines

Construct a time line in the classroom. Cover a large 4' x 8' board with burlap. Use heavy yarn or string to divide the board into twelve equal columns. Label

each column with the name of a month. Have each child bring in a picture of himself and put it in the proper column to mark his birthday. As noteworthy events occur during the school year, mark them on the time line. Place a marker on the time line to identify the dates of famous people and occasions that are studied. At the end of the year, children will enjoy looking back at the time-line record of class events. Children may also keep individual time lines to record events in their lives that occurred during the school year.

Paper Growing

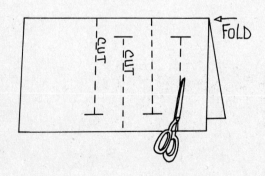

Children fold a sheet of 12″ x 18″ construction paper in half lengthwise. Beginning at either end of the paper, cut a strip 1″ wide almost to the opposite edge. Children stop ½″ before they come to the fold, being careful not to cut through it. Then children turn the paper around and cut another 1″ strip next to the first one. Again, children must be careful not to cut completely through the fold. Children continue cutting, remembering to turn the paper over each time and to stop before they come to an edge. When the entire paper is cut in strips, open it up and pull very gently. Children will be amazed to see the paper "grow."

Daily Dilemmas

Keeping a daily record is an excellent way for children to begin expressing some of their "growing-up" feelings. Review some of the feelings discussed in the poem "Growing Pains." A diary may be kept to record daily "dilemmas" in the classroom, or children may express their feelings in cartoon drawings, poems, or illustrations.

Extra suggestion: Encourage children to keep summer scrapbooks and vacation diaries to record family fun.

Look at Me

Encourage original writing by having children write their autobiographies. Have children include:

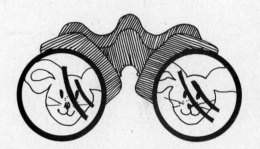

1. The greatest achievement in my life
2. The greatest obstacle in my life
3. The greatest disappointment in my life
4. Twenty years from now (predictions of adult life)
5. Three words that I would like to make famous

From Cubs to Bears

Have children make a list of baby animals. Class decides what that animal will be when it grows up. The list can keep growing.

Cub—Bear
Pony—Horse
Kitten—Cat
Puppy—Dog
Lamb—Sheep
Calf—Cow
Bunny—Rabbit
Fawn—Deer
Duckling—Duck
Piglet—Hog

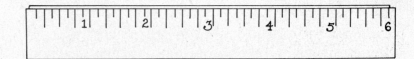

Rods, Rulers, and Reams

Give children plenty of practice with measurement as a way of teaching the concept of growth. Have the children find ways to measure the height of wheat, potato plants, or radish plants grown in the classroom. By experimenting with pencils, thumbs, handspans, and footsteps, children will understand the need for a standard unit of measure. Introduce children to Cuisenaire rods for beginning measurement with metrics. (For example, one rod = one centimeter; ten rods = one decimeter.) Children can quickly see that ten centimeters equal one decimeter.

Introduce meter sticks with centimetric markings. Have children find things that are longer and shorter than the meter stick. Encourage children to predict the lengths of objects *before* they measure. Children compare their estimates with measured results.

Grow Up

At the beginning of the school year, mount large sheets of paper on a board and measure each student, using a meter stick. Mark the height of each child. Toward the end of the year, repeat the measuring process and have children observe growth patterns.

House Plants

Types of Plants. (1) Flowering (have seeds), (2) nonflowering (have spores). All plants have roots.

Plant Regions. (1) Desert plants: cactus, succulents. They do not need much water. (2) Tropical plants: ferns, orchids, philodendron, African violet. They need lots of water. (3) Subtropical plants: poinsettia, azaleas, camelias. These are found in Southern California and Florida and need a medium amount of water.

Experiment:

1. Put any type of small fern in a glass jar. Cover it with a lid. (This creates a tropical environment.)
2. Put the same type of small fern in a pot exposed to open air. Do not cover.
3. Place the two ferns side by side.

Children observe which fern grows best. The fern in the jar will grow best because it represents a miniature tropical environment. (Note: Do not put these plants in direct sunlight.)

Sprinkling Can

Match each plant to the amount of water it needs.

Plant	*How Much Water?*
Cactus	A lot
Fern	
Poinsettia	
Camelia	Medium
Orchid	
Azalea	Very little
Philodendron	

"Growing Pains" by Kari Katzman, age 6

Scrambled Legs

I walk to school and I walk home
All around the town I roam
I can run and I can skip
But many times I fall or trip

Over my familiar shoes
Every day another bruise
Like my early morning eggs
Sometimes I have scrambled legs

"Scrambled Legs" by Janna King, age 11

Grumpy

I wonder why I'm tired out
And dragging at my feet
I wonder why I'm grumpy
And unkind to those I meet

I wonder why I didn't know
The answers on my test
I wonder why I didn't want
The sandwich I like best

I wonder why I shoved my friend
When he got in my way
I wonder why I don't feel good
About the world today

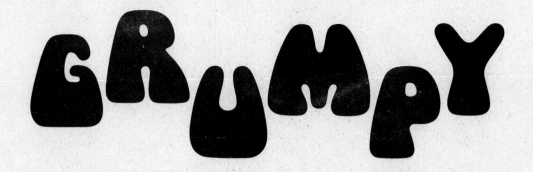

STARTERS AND STRETCHERS

I feel so grumpy today. . . .
My sister/brother keeps bothering me. . . .
My mother doesn't understand. . . .
My friend doesn't want to play. . . .

EXTENDERS

Grumpy Gab Session

Topics to be included: When are you grumpy? How do you feel inside? Grumpy is a *feeling*. Everyone feels that way sometimes.

Vocabulary Building: Grumpy Talk

Sad   Frustrated
Angry   Tired
Lonely   Confused

When you are grumpy, do you want to be left alone? Can other people sometimes help you get over your grumpy feeling? What can you do if the grumpy feeling won't go away?

A Grumpy Sign

Experiment to find out which colors look grumpy. Are you feeling grumpy today? "I am feeling grumpy today—how can I make it go away?"

Set up a "Grumpy Corner" in the classroom. Children design their own "grumpy" signs to hang in the corner. Provide small pillows. Encourage children to go sit in this spot if they have a grumpy feeling. Provide paper for children to draw their grumpy feelings. They may choose scribble or realistic drawing. The "Grumpy T-Shirt" tear sheet on page 188 may be kept in the "Grumpy Corner." Children may share their drawings or throw them away.

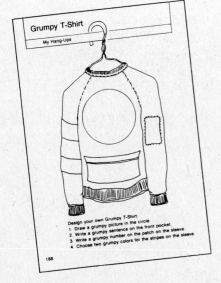

A Grumpy T-Shirt

Use the tear sheet on page 188 to create individual grumpy garments. Duplicate the "Grumpy T-Shirt" on construction paper. Choose appropriate colors, words, pictures, numbers, and sentences to complete the shirt.

Have children design their own "Grumpy T-Shirt":

1. Draw a grumpy picture in the circle.
2. Write a grumpy sentence on the front pocket.
3. Write a grumpy number on the patch on the sleeve.
4. Choose two grumpy colors for the stripes on the other sleeve.

Extra suggestion: T-shirts may be duplicated and redesigned to reflect any mood.

T-Shirt Center

In a corner of the classroom, open a "T-shirt shop" and display children's individualized shirts in the "store window" on a bulletin board or an easel. Have each child put a price tag on his shirt. Children may write their names on the back. Give children an opportunity to go on a shopping spree. Let them choose the T-shirt they would like to "buy."

Live Wires

Use a wire coat hanger for each child to "hang up" his feelings. Tie strings to parts of the hanger and attach cards with the child's feelings written on them. A paper circle with a face drawn on it can be mounted on top of the hanger to illustrate the child's expression.

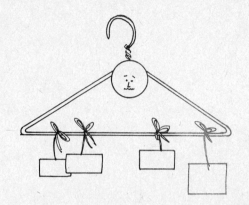

A Mobile of Feelings

Have a private conference with each child and ask him to describe a recent feeling. The children write their feeling on paper of assorted sizes, shapes, and colors. On the reverse side, draw a picture to represent the feeling. Punch holes in the cards and tie a string to each. Hang cards from hangers or a wooden dowel and suspend from ceiling.

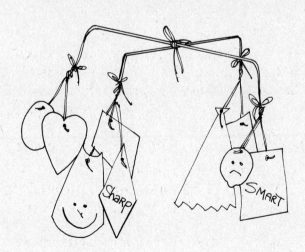

"Grumpy" by Stephen Bronte, age 6

Umbrella Trip

Umbrellas are used to protect us
From the rain or from the sun
But I have an umbrella
That is used to have some fun

When I hold it very high
It pulls me so that I can fly

When I stretch it long and wide
It puts me on a magic ride

When I open it half way
It takes me to another day

And when I close it very tight
I quickly disappear from sight

"Umbrella Trip" by Darcy Troy, age 10

109

Ice Cream–Covered Cure

My stomach hurts
My nose is stuffed
My feet burn when I walk

My sweater's hot
My shoes are tight
My throat hurts when I talk

My blister stings
My hand is cramped
My ears and head both ache

I know the cure
I'll simply make
Some ice cream–covered cake

I ate the cake
My stomach hurt
I ate more than I should

I better find
Some other ways
To make myself feel good

Ice Cream-Covered Cure

STARTERS AND STRETCHERS

Feeling Better? Extend the meaning of the word *cure*. Discuss cure in a *medical sense*. What kinds of cures does a doctor prescribe for colds, flu, or measles? How does the doctor know which cure to prescribe? Discuss cure in a *personal sense*. What can we do to make ourselves feel better:

When you have had a scary dream?
When you missed making an important basket in a basketball game or struck out at bat?
When your best friend moves to a new school?

EXTENDERS

Classroom Cure Cards

Have children decide on a common problem that exists in the classroom. Discuss scarcity as it relates to highly desirable classroom items:

There are not enough checker sets.
There are not enough felt markers.
There are not enough chairs.

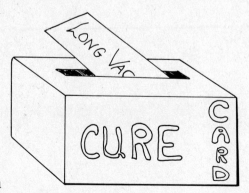

Using folded paper or index cards, children write individual cures to their problems and put them in a box. Problem-solving opportunities occur when children share their solutions, or "cures."

Medical Center

Create a First-Aid Station in the classroom. List first-aid treatment for minor accidents:

> Bruised knee
> Minor cut
> Swollen elbow
> Cut lip
> Splinter

Acquaint children with specialized people who give medical aid:

> Doctor　　　　Orthodontist
> Nurse　　　　Orthopedist
> Dentist　　　　Rescue Squad
> Cardiologist　Lifeguard

Encourage role-playing to motivate learning life-saving techniques. Set up a table with empty medicine bottles, vials, bandages, and splints. Give children opportunities to practice emergency aid in dramatic-play situations.

Note: The first medical school in the United States was established in 1765 at the University of Pennsylvania.

Vocabulary Building: Medical Talk

> Immunization
> Immunity
> Allergy
> Wound
> Penicillin

Sure Cure

Group Analysis. Help children to:

> Identify their feelings
> Understand why these feelings exist
> Think of a cure to make them feel better
> Enjoy the pleasure that comes from solving a problem

Private Prescription. Use the "Sure Cure" tear sheet on page 189. Define the words:

Diagnosis: How do you feel today?
Consultation: Why?
Prescription: What to do?
Cure: Results? Are you cured?

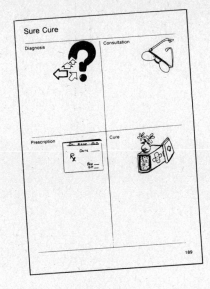

Using the "Sure Cure" tear sheet:

1. Diagnosis: Write a self-diagnosis of their problem. Is it physical or emotional?
2. Consultation: Discuss the problem with the doctor.
3. Prescription: Imagine the doctor's prescription. Write it down.
4. Cure: Write the results.

Note: Remember the bear in the poem "Ice Cream–Covered Cure"? Did he choose the best prescription for his problems? Was he cured?

Health Habits

How can our physical health affect our feelings and emotional health? Use the "Tasty Tree" tear sheet on page 180. Have children illustrate foods emphasizing proper diet on the branches of the tree.

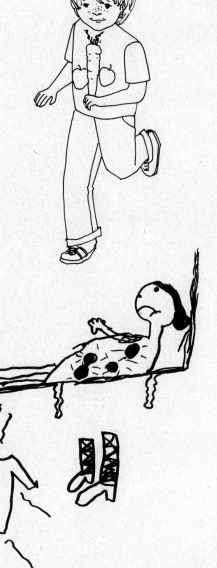

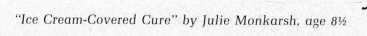

"Ice Cream-Covered Cure" by Julie Monkarsh, age 8½

Stomach Ache

Take a cup of marshmallows
One purple jelly bean
Forty-seven candy bars
And peanuts in between

Mix it with bananas
Put it on the heat
Wait for fifteen minutes
And then begin to eat

It seems this tasty recipe
Is guaranteed to make
Dessert for twenty people
And a great big stomach ache

Stomach Ache

STARTERS AND STRETCHERS

Write your own stomach ache recipe.

"Stomach Ache à la ___(name)___."

Three scoops of _____.
Four sour _____.
One sweet _____ on top.
Mix with _____ syrup.
Add one cup chopped _____.
One tablespoon _____.
Two tablespoons _____.
Four teaspoons _____.
A dash of _____ and _____.
A very tiny pinch of _____.
Combine ingredients. Mix well. Eat.

EXTENDERS

Vocabulary Building: Kitchen Talk

Acquaint children with culinary terms:

Bake	Broil	Brew	Braise	Blend
Boil	Simmer	Fry	Sauté	Purée

Print-a-Pancake

Prepare pancake batter using a packaged mix. Lightly grease a skillet and heat. Pour pancake mix onto skillet in the shape of alphabet letters. Allow time to brown and then turn over. Permit children to choose the letters they want to eat.

115

I Forgot

I left my spelling book at school
I lost my new brown coat

I couldn't find my notebook
I lost the poem I wrote

I put the wrong date on the test
It's August not September

I guess I really need to know
If I WANT to remember

I FORG T

STARTERS AND STRETCHERS

Who Am I? I woke up one morning and lost my memory. I couldn't remember who I was. So I decided to be another person.

What is my name?
Where do I live?
How old am I?
What year is it?
What is my occupation or job?

Write a story or poem about this imaginary person. Draw a picture of this person. (*Suggestion:* I may live in another country or on another planet.)

EXTENDERS

Forget-Me-Nots

A forget-me-not is a plant with fuzzy leaves and many small blue and white flowers. It is considered an emblem of friendship.

I want my friend to remember _____.
I want my teacher to remember _____.
I want my mother to remember _____.

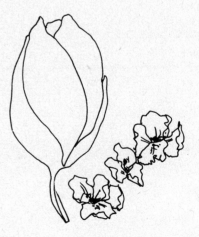

Elephants and Dodo Birds

The elephant never forgets; the Mauritius dodo couldn't remember. The dodo was the first bird to become extinct in modern times. It was a sluggish bird that couldn't fly. The last dodo vanished at the end of the seventeenth century.*

Using the "I Always Remember" tear sheet on page 190, write words, numbers, names, phrases, and colors in spaces provided on the elephant. In the section called, "I Always Forget," write words, numbers, names, phrases, and colors in space provided around the question mark.

Extra suggestions for tear sheet:

I usually forget _____.
I feel sad when I forget _____.
I feel happy when I forget _____.
I feel sorry when I forget _____.
I feel confused when I forget _____.

Lost and Found

Fill in the "forgotten" words in the sentence: "I was surprised to see _____ because I thought he was _____." Have children create their own sentences, "forgetting" key words. Children can exchange papers and have their friends "remember" the missing words.

Spelling Stumpers

Have children submit spelling lists, omitting one letter from each word. Have children exchange papers, fill in the missing letters, and write the words correctly.

*Reference: Roger Troy Peterson and the Editors of Time-Life Books, *The Birds* (New York: Time-Life, 1968).

Homemade Rules

I don't know why
I must get dressed
And go to school today

I don't know why
I can't stay home
And sit around and play

If I stayed home I'd walk outside
Without my shoes and socks

I'd wear my old torn blue jeans
And go collecting rocks

I'd play some games with anyone
And always be the winner

I'd have a Coke at breakfast time
And candy bars for dinner

I'd take a hike while all the kids
Were working hard at school

And wouldn't have to worry
About breaking any rule

Lazy

I like to do so many things
I like to run and go
To a party or a picnic
A movie or a show

I like to ride my bicycle
I like to rollerskate
But sometimes I'm so busy
That I hurry and I'm late

Sometimes I keep moving
Just like a spinning top
I think I need a little time
To just unwind and stop

To take a while for dreaming
And let myself feel hazy
Not to have a thing to do
It's nice to just be lazy

LAZY

STARTERS AND STRETCHERS

I can think of so many lazy words: _____.
I feel lazy when I see these colors: _____.

Use the "Lazy Language" tear sheet on page 191.
(1) Write "lazy" words on the large segments of
the turtle shell. (2) Draw "lazy" colors in the small
segments of the turtle shell.

Extra suggestion: Children may use line design
and color to design their own imaginary turtle.

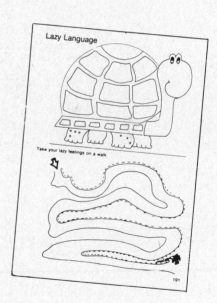

EXTENDERS

Take Your Lazy Feelings on a Walk

Using the "Lazy Language" tear sheet, have children
write a "lazy" story or poem within the lines of the
path. Children should be encouraged not to worry
about spelling, handwriting, or punctuation. They
may even wish to write some words upside down.

Extra for Experts: Perfect the story—punctuation,
spelling, etc.

My Friend

I can whisper secret schemes
And tell about my private dreams

I can share a silly thought
Or talk about the game I bought

And I can shout when I am mad
Or even cry when I feel sad

I show my feelings, real or pretend
When I'm with my special friend

Can't Wait

I can't wait 'til tomorrow
I'm going to the zoo
I can't wait 'til next Tuesday
I have something else to do

I can't wait 'til next Sunday
I'm going to a show
I can't wait 'til next Monday
I have someplace else to go

What's the hurry, what's the rush
Tomorrow's far away
I think I'll wait for things to come
And just enjoy Today

Perfect

I'm just perfect
I'm the best
I do so well
On every test

But I don't really
Want to be
Doing things
So perfectly

It's true that I am very proud
When perfect grades I earn
But when I make a few mistakes
I'll look at them and learn

I'm glad that I'm not perfect
For now I really see
That I cannot expect so much
Of you, my friend, or me

PERFECT

STARTERS AND STRETCHERS

The person I admire most _____.
I would most like to be _____.
My friends like me because _____.
I am different from my sisters and brothers
because _____.
When I grow up, I will be happy if _____ .
I know I am not perfect because _____ .

EXTENDERS

Walk a Perfect Line

Draw a straight line across the room. Each player is
given a pair of binoculars. He looks through the
large lens (the lines will appear small and distorted).
Player must keep his heel and toe on the line as he
walks and looks through the binoculars. It is much
harder than it seems!

Line Up for Friendship

Have the class compile a list of qualities that make a good friend. Write them horizontally across the board with space between the words.

Fair	Sensitive	Energetic
Honest	Sharing	Trusting
Kind	Loyal	Sympathetic
	Dependable	

Have children line up under the quality that best describes the kind of friend they are to other people. To extend the activity, each group forms a committee to represent the friendship quality. After conferring, a spokesperson is chosen from each group to describe the quality, discuss its importance, and tell how it is recognizable in friends.

Pocket Full of Friendship

Design a pocket from construction paper or fabric and attach it to a sheet of tagboard. Have each child write one quality that makes a good friend on a 3″ x 5″ card and put it in the pocket. The contents of the pocket may be emptied and shared with the class.

My Friend Is . . .

Trace a life-sized replica of a child. Have a child lie down on a large piece of butcher paper while another child traces around him. Cut out the drawing and mount it on the wall. Paint in face, clothing, and body details. Attach a sign around the neck, "My Friend Is." Use the cards taken from the "Pocket Full of Friendship." Paste them all over the figure. Give children opportunities to comment on the qualities of their friends.

The People I Admire . . .

Use pictures of people children admire cut from magazines. Choose personalities from many walks of life (sports, entertainment, politics, etc.). Children may draw people they know and admire. Children identify their person and write a description of why they hold this person in high esteem. Discuss the fact that even these people can make mistakes.

Nice Things We Did—A Bulletin Board

Take a moment each day to evaluate class activities and decide on some good things that happened in school. Record each idea on a strip of paper. Be sure to include cognitive and affective learnings.

> "Jeff helped John paint the car."
> "Jill learned a new word."
> "Lora, Kari, and Stephen taught the class a new game."

This is an excellent opportunity to give recognition to all learners of their accomplishments. Children will begin to recognize the positive situations that occur in the classroom. How did each child try his best?

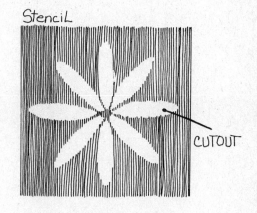

Perfect Images

Have children create "perfect" images by making stencils.

Stencil: Draw a simple design on construction paper as shown in the diagram. Cut it out with X-acto knife or scissors.

Print: Tape stencil to a sheet of white construction paper. Sponge-paint the open spaces. Remove tape. A perfect image is created.

Calligraphy Comments

Beautiful handwriting is an art form. This art form is called *calligraphy.** The styles shown in the illustration are italic, script, and roman. Italic is the simplest for children to learn. Black markers can be used. Children enjoy learning about calligraphy and are fascinated with their own ability.

SUGGESTED SOURCE BOOK

Viorst, Judith. *Alexander and the No Good, Very Bad Day.* New York: Atheneum, 1972. After sharing the story, guide the discussion to help children discover that everyone, everywhere, has days that are not perfect—even in Australia.

*Reference: Charles Stoner and Henry Frankenfield, eds., *Speedball Textbook for Pen and Brush Lettering*, 20th ed. (Philadelphia: Hunt Manufacturing, 1972).

Compare

You are cold
I am hot

You are smart
I am not

You are calm
I am mad

You are good
I am bad

Why compare with others
In a game or on a test

I think it's more important
To simply do my best

COMPARE

STARTERS AND STRETCHERS

Comparing Feelings:
Cold/Hot
Smart/Dumb
Calm/Mad
Good/Bad

When did you feel this way?
How long did the feeling last?
What made the feeling go away?

EXTENDERS

Let's Compare: A Three-Step Process

Young children can begin collecting information, sorting data, drawing conclusions, and making comparisons. Representing a comparison pictorially permits the child to see the relationships between things.

Step 1: Surveys. Have children compile a list of information that they want to find out about each other. The list would include: birthdays, addresses, heights, weights. In addition, the list could include each child's favorite:

Foods	Music	Television programs
Cars	Animals	Shoes
Games	Books	Art media
Toys	Movies	Pets

129

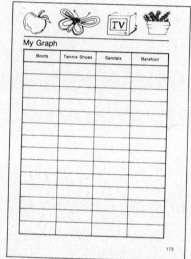

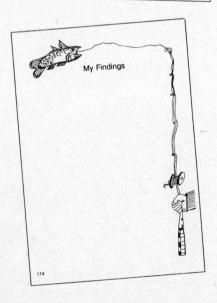

Encourage the children to be imaginative in their choice of survey topics.

Have each child choose one topic from the list for his survey. Use the "My Survey" tear sheet on page 172. Have the children write the type of survey they are conducting and then list several categories at the top of each column. Children interview members of the class. Each child indicates his response by signing his name in the appropriate column of the survey sheet.

A "Favorite Shoe" survey might include these categories:

> Tennis Shoes
> Boots
> Sandals
> Barefoot

When each child is ready to interview his friends, he reads the choices and records the responses in the appropriate column.

Step 2: Graphs. When the surveys are completed, children record and communicate their experiences on a bar graph. Children count the number of responses in each of their survey categories. Young children may use Cuisenaire rods to make a visual picture of the information. Use the "My Graph" tear sheet on page 173 to record the results of the surveys. Color the correct number of spaces to match the survey results. Use a different-colored crayon for each column.

Step 3: Interpretations. When the information is recorded, children will begin to interpret and make comparisons. This information is recorded on the "My Findings" tear sheet on page 174. The findings for the shoe survey might include some of the following interpretations:

1. Most of my friends like tennis shoes.
2. No one likes _____.
3. Few people like sandals the best.

All the findings sheets may be bound in a class book. An appropriate title might be added: "Things We Found Out about Our Friends."

Positive and Negative Space

Demonstrate the effect of contrast. Suggested media: crayon or crayon resist. Have children fold an 11″ x 14″ paper in half. Label one half "Positive Space"; label the other half "Negative Space."

Children draw an object (chair, lamp, etc.) in the "Positive Space." They use line design to decorate the object (five colors or more). The background ("Negative Space") is left blank. Children draw the same object again in the "Negative Space." This time, design is used only in the background "Negative Space," using the same colors that were used in the "Positive Space" drawing. Compare and contrast the images in the "Positive" and "Negative" spaces. (The object or shape is the positive space. The background is the negative space.) Positive and negative space are basic elements in pictorial composition.

Scissors-Happy

Fold small sheets of colored paper in half. Cut half a shape along the fold (heart, diamond, etc.). Remove the cut-out section. Open the folded paper. Mount it on contrasting paper (the part that was cut away is negative space). Experiment with different sizes and shapes.

Picture This

The teacher collects small actual objects. Next the teacher reads the directions and specifications for the objects children are to draw on their papers. For example, the teacher might direct the children to draw:

A circle: the size of a Lifesaver
A line: the length of a stick of gum
A rectangle: the size of a playing card
A circle: the size of a bottle top
A line: the length of a spoon
A line: the length of a paper towel roll
An oval: the size of an egg

When children have drawn and labelled the objects, they compare them—first with each other's drawings and then with the actual object. This activity reinforces visual memory.

Map Measures

Have children make maps of the classroom. Use large sheets of newsprint. Label directions: north, south, east, and west. Indicate doors, windows, chalkboards, bookshelves, closets, tables, chairs, desks, bulletin boards, and learning centers. Encourage children to develop legends for their maps, using symbols to represent objects. Have children continue their map-making at home. Instruct them to make a map of their bedroom, kitchen, living room, dining room, or playroom. Children can bring their maps of home to school to be shared and compared.

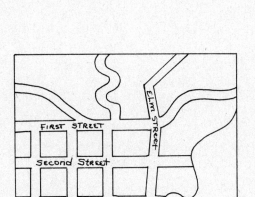

Map the Neighborhood. Draw a street map of the area where your school is located. Include street names and important landmarks. Pin the map on a bulletin board. As each child learns to say his address correctly, have him pin a small cutout of his house on the appropriate spot on the map.

Design appropriate research questions for the map center:

How many children live on Elm Drive?
How many children live *west* of Oak Street?
How many children live on the same street as the post office?
Find *your* house. Give the names of your two *nearest* neighbors.
Name all of the children who live *between* school and Oak Street.

SUGGESTED SOURCE BOOK

Lionni, Leo. *Inch by Inch.* New York: Ivan Obolensky, 1960. A delightful story and pictures depicting the adventures of an inchworm. Have children create inchworms of their own for use in measuring. Use colored construction paper. Children design inchworms and add details.

It's Not Fair

My mother said I could not go
Your mother said you could
You didn't want to play the game
I said I really would

I had to walk to school today
My sister got a ride
My friends went to the park to play
I had to stay inside

My teacher said I talked in school
I didn't say a thing
The class all laughed at music time
I didn't get to sing

I told my friend I liked him
He said he didn't care
I shook my head and told myself
I think that it's not fair!

Secret

My friend told me a secret
She said, "Oh, please don't tell"
I promised that I wouldn't
I keep secrets very well

I really liked the secret
It seemed just like a present
But it became too big for me
And I felt quite unpleasant

Now I want to give it out
And whisper it to you
Keeping any secret
Is hard for me to do

SECRET

STARTERS AND STRETCHERS

Top Secret. Write a story using primitive picture symbols. Children can design their own symbols to represent words. Examples:

Tooth	Eye
Tree	Hand
House	

EXTENDERS

Indian Sign Language

Early in the morning I saw the bright _____.
I walked on a _____ and saw a _____
and a _____. I followed a _____. I sat
on a _____. It started to rain and became
very dark. I saw _____ and _____ in
the sky. Then I came home to my _____.

The American Indians of the plains and lakes had
their own special symbolic language. The symbols
below represent the graphic expressions of their
daily lives.* Children will enjoy reproducing these
Indian symbols and writing sign-language messages
to each other.

*References: Gyorgy Kepes, ed., *Sign, Image, Symbol* (New York:
George Braziller, 1966); Leroy H. Appleton, *American Indian Design
and Decoration* (New York: Dover, 1971).

Private Eye

Give children:

A list of misspelled words.
A sentence with incorrect punctuation.
A story with misspelled words and incorrect punctuation.

Children proofread and correct the errors.

Extra suggestion: Children write their own stories with misspelled words and other errors. They exchange papers with other children and correct the mistakes.

Pen Names

Staple sheets of blank newsprint together with a cover of construction paper. The children decorate the covers of their books. Each child collects autographs from his friends, teachers, and parents. Special visitors to school may be asked to sign the book.

Secret Codes

This is a writing activity for a small group of children. The teacher calls out five letters of the alphabet—for example, *g, l, p, r, m.* Children write the letters in a column on the left-hand side of their paper. Now children are ready to construct a sentence by using the five letters in the order in which they were called to begin each new word in the sentence. (Example: *Girls love pretzels, raisins, marshmallows.*) As children become more adept at writing sentences, increase the number of letters given.

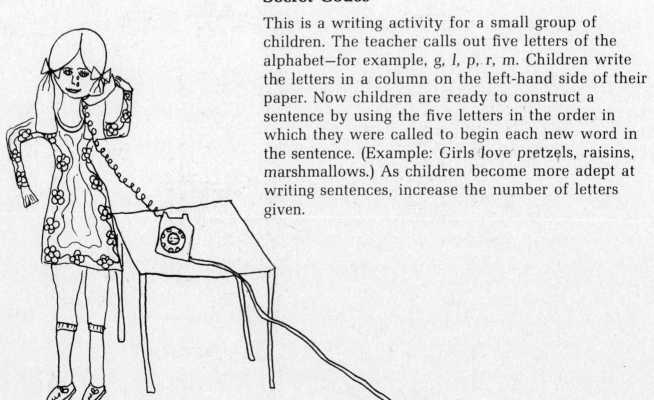

"Nobody's There" by Cathy Donnerstag, age 9

Nobody's There

I called my friend Katie
She was out for a walk
I called my friend Danny
But he couldn't talk

I called my friend Stephie
She was playing with Mark
I called my friend Lainie
She went to the park

I called all my friends
Doesn't anyone care
I feel so alone
Because nobody's there

Share

Sometimes I like to share my things
With someone whom I know
Sometimes I like to hide my things
Away where they won't show

It's nice to keep things private
Just for my very own
But sometimes I can get to feel
So quiet and alone

And that's the time I need a friend
To wonder and compare
Because it really can be fun
To bring things out and share

SHARE

STARTERS AND STRETCHERS

Help Wanted: "A person to help me with my
_____ (multiplication tables, spelling words,
art project, science report). Please contact
_____ (name) in person as soon as possible."

Have children place their messages on a "Want Ad"
bulletin board.

EXTENDERS

Share Sessions

Each child chooses a partner. Give each team of
two, ten minutes to share everything they want to
know about each other (likes, dislikes, middle
names, sisters, brothers, pets). Call the class together
again and ask each child to tell what he learned
about his partner. Can he remember? Did he listen?
This is an excellent way for children to get to know
each other at the beginning of the school year.

Sign Up to Share

Designate a section of the chalkboard where
children can write their names when they want to
share something with the class. Set aside time

during the day or week when sharing activities may be enjoyed. The teacher might suggest weekly themes to encourage relevance in materials brought to school. Some suggested topics:

Book Week
Favorite Color Week
Stuffed Animal Week
Favorite Jewelry or Accessory Week
Favorite Pastime or Hobby Week
Poster Week
Favorite Toy Week
Favorite Clothes Week
Favorite Television Program Week
Favorite Food Week

Pass the Poetry

Children will enjoy sharing in writing their own poems. A small group of children sit in a circle, each with his own sheet of paper. On the top line, a child writes one line of an original poem. (The teacher may determine the subject.) Then the child folds the paper down so the top line is no longer visible. At the signal, he passes it to the child on his right. He whispers the last word of his line to the child as he passes the paper. Without peeking, the next child adds a line of his own, making sure the last word rhymes with the line above. This continues until the paper has circulated once around the circle. The poem will have as many lines as there are children in the circle. When the poem reaches the first poet, it is opened and shared by all.

Trading Post

A small group of children sits in a circle. Each child has a sheet of paper and a pencil. On the top line of the paper, the child writes the first line of a story. (The teacher may structure this.)

I took a magic carpet ride to India. . . .
I got in my rocket and blasted off to the moon. . . .
I really enjoyed my birthday party this year. . . .

When the children complete their story openers, the teacher gives a signal and each child passes his paper to the child on his right. Encourage children to read the previous sentence carefully and then add an original sentence that continues the story and has meaning. Continue the process of passing the stories, reading the previous sentences, and creating a new sentence. When the story returns to the first author, children share the completed text. Post the stories on the bulletin board.

Hands-On Mural

Each child creates a drawing of anything he wishes (no special theme). Next, divide the class into four or five groups. Through discussion, children share ideas and develop an imaginative theme from their pictures. After a theme is established, children may begin to draw a mural on a long sheet of paper. They may use ideas from their original drawings. The project may continue over a period of time.

Extra suggestion: Several children can work together on a smaller sheet of paper and design a miniature mural.

Vocabulary Building: Art Composition Concepts

How can the mural be improved? Encourage children to discuss the following art concepts as the mural develops:

Color (contrast)	Shapes
Content	Size (variety)
Design	Dimension

SUGGESTED SOURCE BOOK

Hill, Elizabeth Starr. *Evan's Corner*. New York: Holt, Rinehart and Winston, 1967. Illustrated by Nancy Grossman. Children will enjoy hearing the sensitive story of Evan and his discovery of a special place of his own. After children have heard the story, have them design special corners of their own. Use lines drawn in perspective to create, a corner. Children write their name over the corner: "Jon's Corner." Children draw or cut out pictures of special objects for their corner:

Furniture	Toys
Rug	Pets
Windows	Food

"Share" by Vanda Puhalovich, age 6

"Share" by Gary Blond, age 7

A Special Day

Birthdays are special
And Valentine's Day
Christmas, Thanksgiving
The first day of May

Getting a costume
When it's Halloween
But what do we do
On the days in between

A day can be special
By the friends that I meet
Or taking a walk
Down a beautiful street

Or watching a flower
Beginning to grow
Or giving a smile
To someone I know

A day can be special
In some kind of way
What can I do
That is special today?

STARTERS AND STRETCHERS

Greetings. Design a greeting card for any special day:

> Thinking of You
> Get Well
> Write Soon
> Let's Be Friends
> Happy Birthday
> Wish You Were Here

Suggested materials for cards:

Shiny paper	Ribbon
Fabric	Colored construction paper
Wallpaper	Shells
Glitter	Feathers

Make materials available for instant celebrations of important occasions.

EXTENDERS

Birthday Graph

On a large sheet of tagboard, write the name of the month in a column on the left-hand side. An appropriate color and symbol can be used for each

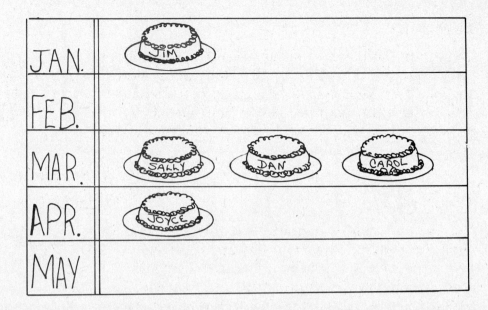

month. Give each child his own "cut-out cake" to record his name and date of birth. Have children place "birthday cakes" next to the appropriate month.

Gift Shopping

Children make lists of special people. Use magazines and catalogues to cut out pictures of gifts for people on the list. Label the gift and tell whom it is for.

News Wrap-Up

Create "ecological" (recycled)) wrapping paper from old newspapers. Spread out a sheet of newspaper. Use thick, colored markers to draw bold letters and designs on the newsprint. Black marker may be used as an accent.

Month-End Posters

To summarize the events of the month, have children design month-end posters. On a large sheet of art paper, write the name of the month in many styles, positions, angles, media. Use line designs and geometric shapes to complete the poster with notable events of the month.

Love Bugs

Have children collect rocks of assorted sizes. Paint the rocks. Use stripes and polka dots. Spray with shellac. With glue, add plastic eyes, pipe cleaner bits, or paint on features. "Love Bugs" make excellent paperweights and special Valentine's Day gifts.

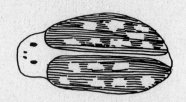

Love Links

Design your own love chain from opened paper clips. An opened paper clip has an "S" shape. Attach paper clips to each other by twisting to secure each clip. Continue until desired length is reached for necklace or bracelet. A wire symbol may be created to hang from the chain.

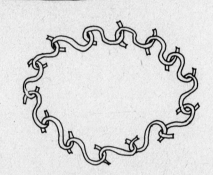

Special Days

Our Country: Study American family traditions. How did an American great grandmother observe special holidays?

Other Countries: Do research for information on holidays and festivities in other countries.

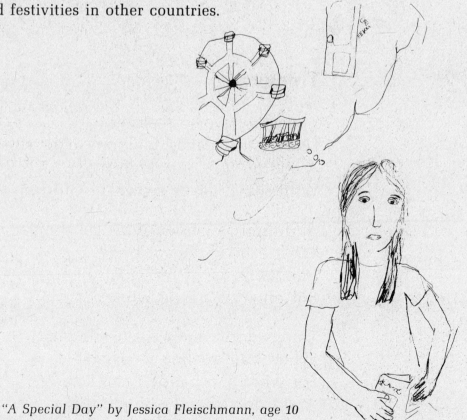

"A Special Day" by Jessica Fleischmann, age 10

Things

I love to have so many things
Like castles, cakes, balloons, and rings
A million toys, a golden tree
With silver leaves grown just for me

And then I wonder, what's a thing
What exactly does it bring
I know it makes me laugh or smile
But only for a little while

Things don't really make me glad
When I am feeling very sad
For when I'm happy I can sing
And I don't need a single thing

Things

STARTERS AND STRETCHERS

"Things" Catalogue:

Old things	Big things
New things	Little things
Happy things	Funny things
Sad things	Scary things

"Things" can be objects or events that have happened. Children use their imaginations and invent categories of their own.

EXTENDERS

Who Am I?

This is an activity for a small group of children. Each child writes two lists: "Things I Like," "Things I Dislike." Lists are collected and read aloud. Everyone has a chance to guess whose list has been read.

Note: Children should have the opportunity to know each other fairly well before playing this game.

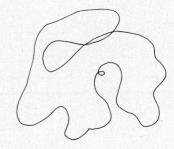

Scribble Drawing

Close your eyes. Use a crayon to scribble over a large sheet of art paper. Open your eyes. How many "things" do you see hidden in your crayon design?

149

Use different-colored crayons to fill in details of objects on your crayon drawing.

Extra suggestion: Repeat the process, making a large scribble drawing. What does the whole scribble represent—an animal, a person, a house? Shapes and design may be added to complete the drawing.

All Kinds of Things

Use 8″ x 10″ plywood boards with grain. See how many "things" you can find in the lines of the grain. Use a pencil to outline shapes, animals, people, plants, trees, and scenes that you find. Use a black marker to outline the important lines, shapes, and designs. Use crayon to add color and detail. Paint the entire surface of the board with one or two watercolor paints. When dry, spray the board with a high-gloss varnish.

Thing Machine

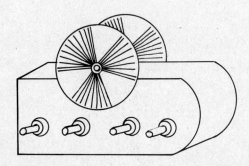

Use your imagination to design a unique, imaginary, fantastic "Thing Machine." Allow plenty of opportunity for group discussion. Give children small scraps of wood and bits of junk. Allow them to create their own machines. Encourage them to show "things" that are produced by their machines. Some possible "Thing Machines":

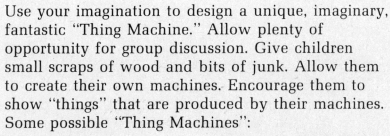

Dress Machine	Candy Machine
Toy Machine	Monster Machine
Bubble Gum Machine	Make-Believe Machine
Sports Machine	Wind Machine

The children will have many suggestions of their own. Apply paint and spray when completed. Set up a museum to display the machines. For added motivation, show the class the illustration on the poem "Things."

150

Can't Decide

I have a day and it is mine
A big long day of open time

Not a crowded busy day
With many things to do and say

I have all the time to use
In any way I pick or choose

I wonder what to do with it
Should I stand or should I sit

Should I read or take a ride
Oh, I really can't decide

Should I plan my day with care
Allowing me no time to spare

Or should I use a lock and key
To tightly close the day from me

Maybe I'll just wait and see
What the day will bring to me

Inside Out

Yesterday a man came by
And took me to the zoo
He put me in a fancy cage
With lots of things to do

The animals all wandered by
They had to pay a dime
Just to stand and look at me
As I would swing and climb

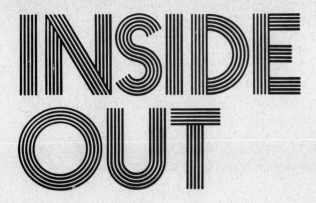

INSIDE OUT

STARTERS AND STRETCHERS

Animal Match-Up. Where do they live?

Bear	Lair
Chicken	Coop
Rabbit	Hutch
Pig	Sty
Bee	Hive
Spider	Web

Scramble the lists and have the children match the animals with their homes.

EXTENDERS

Animal Stuffing

Have children cut out an animal from a large sheet of art paper. It can be real or make-believe. When each child has achieved the desired shape, ask him to cut out another one identical to the first. Draw in details of both animals with markers. Punch holes around the edge. Lace with colored yarn. When three-fourths finished, stuff with cotton and complete the lacing. Encourage children to use imagination.

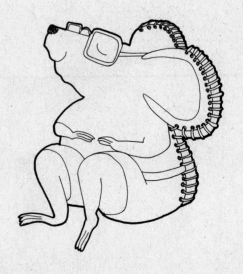

Talk to the Animals

Each child assumes the role of an animal. Use a tape recorder and have children record their "animal thoughts" and impressions of people. Design costumes and pantomime various movements while playing back the recorded thoughts and impressions.

Example: "I wish someone would open my cage." "I wish someone would take me for a walk."

A-Maz-Ing Insects

1. Motivate by showing the work of artist M. C. Escher. His work shows optical illusion, disequilibrium (off balance), upside down, inside out.
2. Children draw a maze. They can use geometric shapes or any type of maze.
3. Children draw various insects in the maze. Drawings can be realistic or fantasy.
4. Children use color and line design for the maze, the shapes, and the insects. They might use a dark color for contour lines.

"Dreams" by Stephanie Fleischmann, age 13

Dreams

At night when I am sleeping
I might begin to dream
Of Princesses and Princes
Drinking chocolate milk and cream

And sometimes I'm an artist
Or a poet or a witch
And I can stay the way I am
Or simply make a switch

Other times I have a dream
That I don't really like
And I awaken suddenly
Bewildered by my fright

I know that all these different dreams
My sleeping mind can make
Are over in the morning
When I am wide awake

Some dreams I like to keep inside
Just like a hidden treasure
And think about them sometimes
Because they give me pleasure

Wishing Phone

I'd like to have a wishing phone
That I could call my very own

And I could dial nine or two
And all my wishes would come true

And if I dial number four
A zillion toys would crowd my floor

And if I dial number one
A funny magic clown would come

And if I dial number nine
A hot fudge sundae would be mine

And if I dial number five
All my friends would soon arrive

And if I want to be alone
I could just hang up the phone

WISHING PHONE

STARTERS AND STRETCHERS

Wishful Thinking. Write an imaginary phone number. Tell what wish came true as you dialed each number.

EXTENDERS

Dial-A-Wish

The telephone company is cooperative about providing actual telephones and bells. Telephones are placed on opposite sides of the room. Each child creates a wishing phone number, containing seven numbers representing seven wishes. Example: 454-7132.

> 4 = "I wish to go to the zoo."
> 7 = "I wish to _____."

The child writes these wishes on a piece of paper or a memo pad. One child at a time places a "call" symbolizing his wishes. Another child receives the "call" (the "wish-receiver") and determines which of the seven wishes will come true.

Instant Replay

Cut out a large replica of a telephone. Place it in the corner of the classroom. Keep a tape recorder or cassette player nearby for each person to "dial" and record his own wish. Play back all the wishes and decide which are possible or impossible.

Wishful Writing

Read the poem "Happy Thought" by Robert Louis Stevenson. This poem was written in 1885.

"The world is so full of a number of things
I'm sure we should be happy as Kings . . ."

Illustrate the "things" that would make us "happy as kings":

"If I had three wishes. . . ."
"A magic genie came into my room last night. I told him. . . ."
"Some wishes that have come true. . . ."

Each child writes five wishes for himself at the beginning of the school year. Collect the wishes. At the end of the year, pass back the wishes to see if they came true. Are they still wished for?

Hidden Treasures

Have each child write his wish on a 3" x 5" index card. Collect the cards, place in a file box, and give children lots of opportunities to read each other's wishes and write additional ones of their own. Visitors to the classroom may be asked to add a card to the file, and the treasure chest can grow all year long.

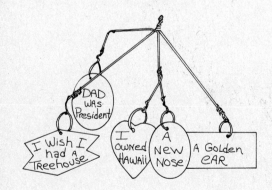

Wishing-Wire Mobile

Children cut colored paper into desired shapes. Write one wish on each shape. Hang shapes from wires that are twisted into interesting designs. Use wire coat hangers or any malleable wire material.

SUGGESTED SOURCE BOOK

Stevenson, Robert Louis. *A Child's Garden of Verse.* New York: Golden Press, 1951.

"Wishing Phone" by Dana Boren, age 11

"Wishing Phone" by Kathy Saffro, age 8½

"Wishing Phone" by Stephanie King, age 9

Chatterbox

I saw a little chatterbox
With arms and legs and head
And it would not stop chattering
Until it went to bed

chatterbox

STARTERS AND STRETCHERS

Voice Volume. Do you:

Whisper	Laugh	Whine
Yell	Squeal	Blabber
Grumble	Mumble	Chatter
Scream	Shriek	Screech

EXTENDERS

Hello! International Chatter

Children learn common salutations in foreign languages. Provide foreign language dictionaries. Children choose a language to research. Set up a miniature United Nations "General Assembly." One child calls out a word or sentence in English. Each child translates the word or sentence into his chosen language.

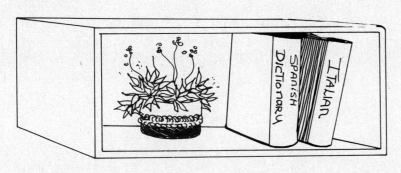

Talk Show

Choose a host or hostess. Invite guests to participate. Select a topic of discussion in advance.

Extra suggestion: Guests may be invited from school staff or community.

Body Language

Children use body movement and appropriate facial expressions to act out a word, a feeling, an object, or an animal. Movement may be expressed in a dance, pantomime, or charade.

Dance Dynamics: Instincts to Share

There is dance all over the world. The way people dance communicates their way of life and thinking. Dancing is considered to be an instinct. We dance in many ways: with joy when something makes us happy, in pain when something hurts us inside or out. If you are with someone who cannot speak your language, your hands dance in a way to help people understand.

The word *dance* comes from an old German word *danson,* which means "to stretch." Dancing is made up of stretching and relaxing. Your muscles tense and then relax as you dance. The various types of dance originate from different countries. Some games we play today relate to dance steps of the past. For example, the game of hopscotch can be traced to an ancient pagan rite. The drawing shows an early hopscotch layout.

Vocabulary Building: Chorus of Complaints

Debate	Suggest
Argue	Rebel
Discuss	Protest
Confer	Petition

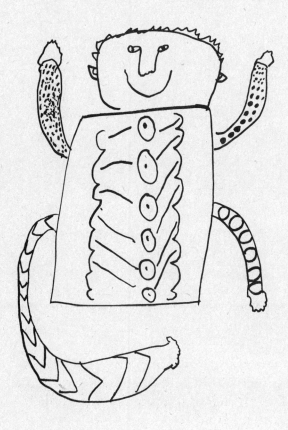

"Chatterbox" by Kari Katzman, age 6

"Chatterbox" by Lynn Lawrence, age 10

Thank You

When I get a present
And smile with delight
It's nice to say "Thank You"
For that is polite

But I can say "Thank You"
In other ways, too
Like showing I care
By nice things that I do

Bibliography

FOR CHILDREN

Aliki (pseud). *My Five Senses.* New York: Thomas Y. Crowell, 1962.

Anderson, Hans Christian. *The Emperor's New Clothes.* New York: Random House, 1971.

Bendick, Jeanne. *The Human Senses.* New York: Franklin Watts, 1968.

Berger, Terry. *I Have Feelings.* New York: Behavioral Press, 1971.

Craig, M. Jean. *The Dragon in the Clock Box.* New York: W. W. Norton, 1962.

Duvoisin, Roger. *House of Four Seasons.* New York: Lothrop, Lee and Shepard, 1956.

Emberly, Ed. *Drawing Book of Animals.* Boston: Little, Brown, 1972.

——. *Make a World.* Boston: Little, Brown, 1972.

Hill, Elizabeth Starr. *Evan's Corner.* New York: Holt, Rinehart and Winston, 1967.

Hoban, Russell. *Bread and Jam for Frances.* New York: Harper and Row, 1964.

Hurd, Edith Thacher. *Wilson's World.* New York: Harper and Row, 1971.

Keats, Ezra Jack. *A Letter to Amy.* New York: Harper and Row, 1968.

Krauss, Ruth. *A Very Special House.* New York: Harper and Row, 1953.

Lionni, Leo. *Inch by Inch.* New York: Ivan Obolensky, 1960.

——. *Little Blue and Little Yellow.* New York: Ivan Obolensky, 1959.

MacAgy, Douglas, and MacAgy, Elizabeth. *Going for a Walk with a Line.* Garden City, N.Y.: Doubleday, 1959.

McGovern, Ann. *Too Much Noise.* Boston: Houghton-Mifflin, 1967.

Madian, John. *Beautiful Junk.* Boston: Little, Brown, 1968.

Montresor, Beni. *House of Flowers, House of Stars.* New York: Alfred A. Knopf, 1962.

O'Neill, Mary. *Hailstones and Halibut Bones.* Garden City, N.Y.: Doubleday, 1961.

Palmer, Helen. *Why I Built the Boogle House.* New York: Beginner Books, 1964.

Podendorf, Illa. *Touching for Telling.* Chicago: Children's Press, 1971.

Saroyan, William. *Me.* New York: Crowell Collier Press, 1963.

Showers, Paul. *Find Out by Touching.* New York: Thomas Y. Crowell, 1961.

——. *Follow Your Nose.* New York: Thomas Y. Crowell, 1963.

FOR TEACHERS

Slepian, Jan, and Seidler, Ann. *The Hungry Thing*. Chicago: Follett, 1967.

Stevenson, Robert Louis. *A Child's Garden of Verse*. New York: Golden Press, 1951.

Viorst, Judith. *Alexander and the No Good, Very Bad Day*. New York: Atheneum, 1972.

Zion, Gene. *Dear Garbage Man*. New York: Harper and Row, 1957.

Appleton, Leroy H. *American Indian Design and Decoration*. New York: Dover, 1971.

Gardner, Helen. *Art through the Ages*, 5th ed. New York: Harcourt, Brace and World, 1970.

Greer, Mary, and Rubinstein, Bonnie. *Will the Real Teacher Please Stand Up?* Santa Monica, Ca: Goodyear, 1972.

Haskell, Arnold L. *The Wonderful World of Dance*. New York: Doubleday, 1969.

Janson, H. W. *History of Art*. Englewood Cliffs, N.J.: Prentice-Hall, and New York: Harry N. Abrams, 1973.

Jung, Carl G. *Man and His Symbols*. New York: Doubleday, 1964.

Kaplan, Sandra N. et al. *Change for Children*. Santa Monica, Ca: Goodyear, 1973.

————. *The Big Book of Writing Games & Activities*. Santa Monica, Ca: Goodyear, 1975.

————. *The Big Book of Collections: Math Games & Activities*. Santa Monica, Ca: Goodyear, 1975.

Kepes, Gyorgy (ed.). *Sign, Image, Symbol*. New York: George Braziller, 1966.

Koch, Kenneth. *Wishes, Lies and Dreams: Teaching Children to Write Poetry*. New York: Random House, Vintage Books/Chelsea House Publishers, 1970.

Lewis, Richard. *Miracles*. New York: Simon and Schuster, 1966.

Lindstrom, Miriam. *Children's Art*. Los Angeles: University of California Press, 1957.

Perrine, Laurence. *Sound and Sense*. New York: Harcourt, Brace, Jovanovich, 1956.

Peterson, Roger Troy, and the Editors of Time-Life Books. *The Birds*. New York: Life Nature Library, 1968.

Pollard, Barbara Kay. *Feelings, Inside You and Outloud Too*. Millbrae, Calif.: Celestial Arts, 1975.

Stoner, Charles, and Frankenfield, Henry (eds.). *Speedball Textbook for Pen and Brush Lettering*, 20th ed. Philadelphia: Hunt Manufacturing, 1972.

4

THE TEAR SHEETS

The tear sheets are special learning devices designed to motivate and reinforce particular activities described in the Creative Experiences. Some of the tear sheets contain specific instructions and are appropriate for use with a large group in a directed activity. Others have been left open-ended and are excellent learning center materials, perfect for individualized activities created by the children or the teacher. All of the tear sheets can be used as open-ended teaching devices simply by taping over undesired instructions or words before duplicating them.

Often, a miniature picture of the tear sheet appears in the Creative Experiences next to its corresponding activity. Each tear sheet is listed by title and page number in the Contents at the front of the book.

People Productions, Inc.

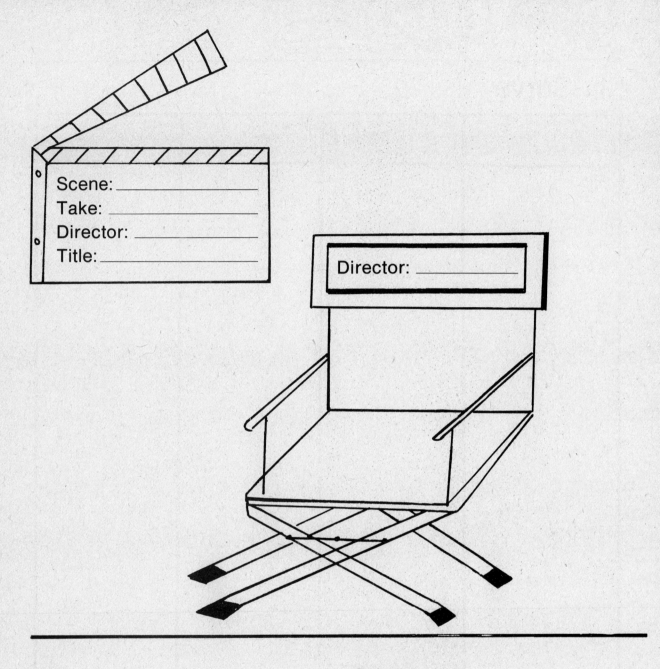

Scene: _____
Take: _____
Director: _____
Title: _____

Director: _____

Title: _____   Screenwriter: _____
Producer: _____   Set Designer: _____
Director: _____   Costume Designer: _____
Cast: _____   Music: _____
    Choreographer: _____
    Cameraperson: _____
    Location: _____

For specific instructions see page 4

My Survey

For specific instructions see pages 129–30

  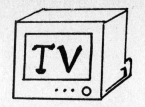 

My Graph

For specific instructions see pages 129–30

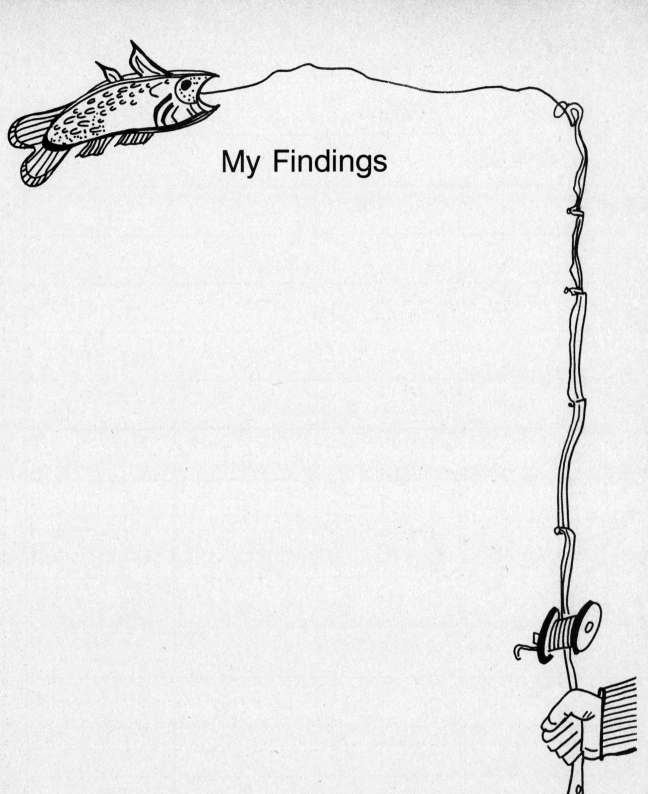

My Findings

For specific instructions see pages 129–30

Word House

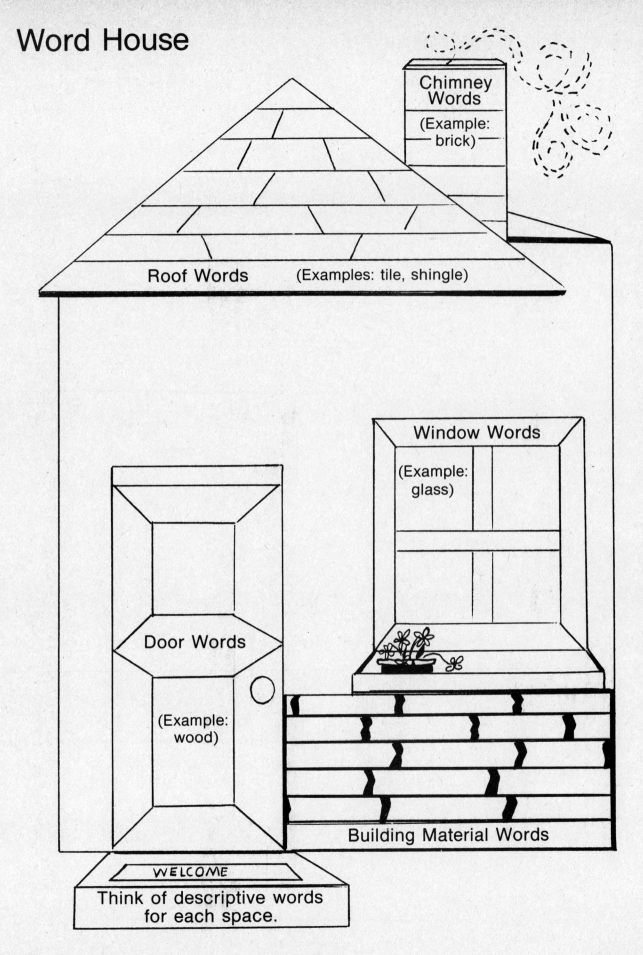

Chimney Words

(Example: brick)

Roof Words   (Examples: tile, shingle)

Window Words

(Example: glass)

Door Words

(Example: wood)

Building Material Words

WELCOME

Think of descriptive words for each space.

For specific instructions see page 28

Color Contraption

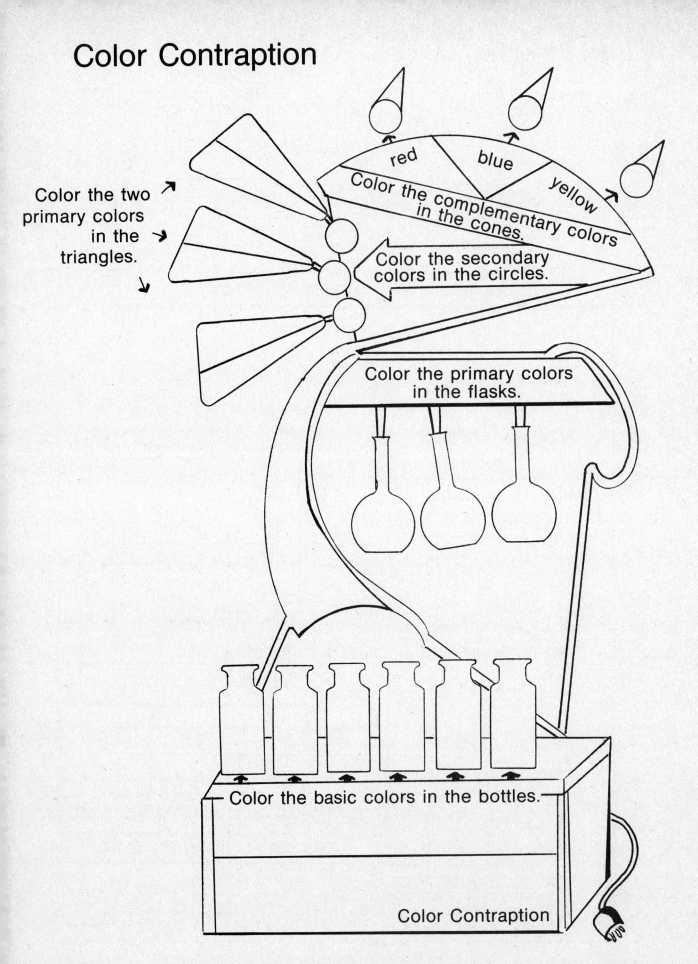

Color the two primary colors in the triangles.

red   blue   yellow

Color the complementary colors in the cones.

Color the secondary colors in the circles.

Color the primary colors in the flasks.

Color the basic colors in the bottles.

Color Contraption

For specific instructions see page 40

Color Coding   Decode the letters and numbers.

Ac2

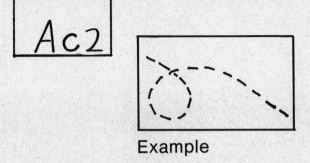

Example

Ba2

Bc1

Aa1

Aa3

Cb2

C3a

Bb3

Shapes		Colors		Line Design	
A	□	a	red	1	〜〜
B	○	b	yellow	2	- - - - -
C	△	c	black	3	∧∧∧∧

For specific instructions see page 40

Mr. Touch-Me

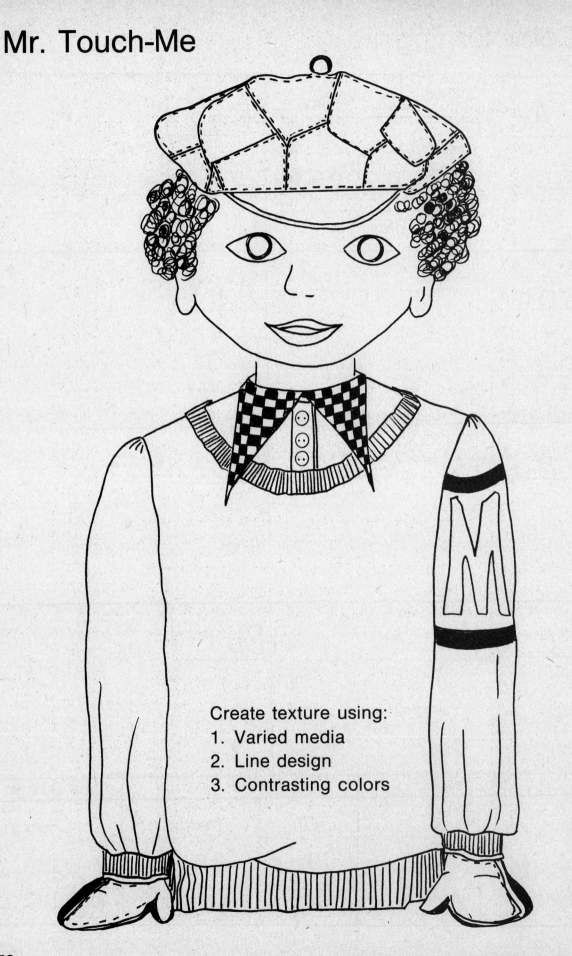

Create texture using:
1. Varied media
2. Line design
3. Contrasting colors

For specific instructions see pages 51–52

THIS TEAR SHEET IS FROM **IMAGINE THAT!** © 1976 GOODYEAR PUBLISHING COMPANY, INC.

Customer Check

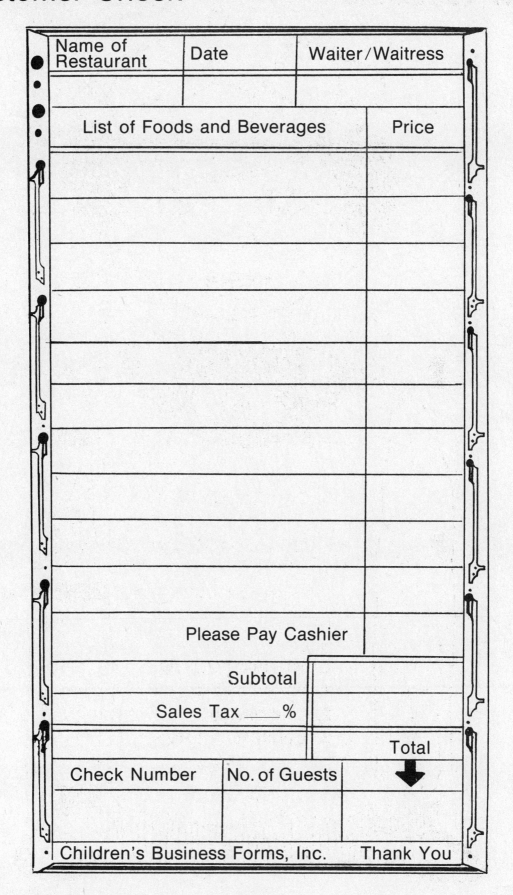

Name of Restaurant	Date	Waiter/Waitress

List of Foods and Beverages	Price

Please Pay Cashier

Subtotal	
Sales Tax ____%	
	Total

Check Number	No. of Guests	↓

Children's Business Forms, Inc.   Thank You

For specific instructions see page 62

Tasty Tree

For specific instructions see page 63

Odor Palette

For specific instructions see page 69

Decorate the Room

Use line design to:
1. Upholster the chair
2. Weave the carpet
3. Decorate the lamp
4. Create an abstract painting

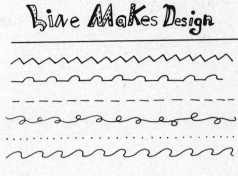

For specific instructions see page 73

Geometric Man
Identify the shapes.

For specific instructions see page 74

Make a Melody

Experiment with sound:
1. Use your voice.
2. Use rhythm instruments.
3. Use parts of your body.
4. Use objects in the room.

Find a sound to accompany each
note on the musical staff:
1. Play a solo.
2. Play a duet.
3. Form a band.
4. Play *forte* (loud).
5. Play *piano* (soft).

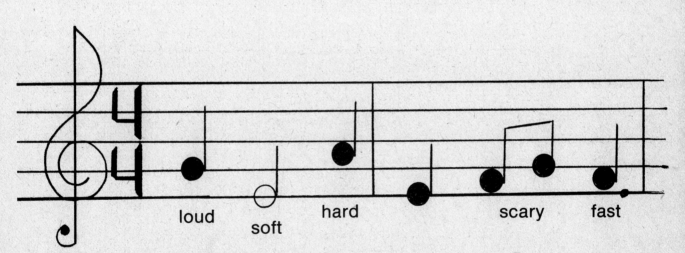

loud   soft   hard   scary   fast

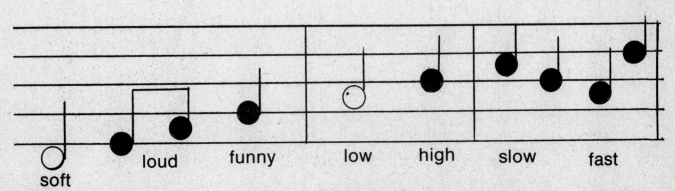

soft   loud   funny   low   high   slow   fast

For specific instructions see page 78

Sales Slip

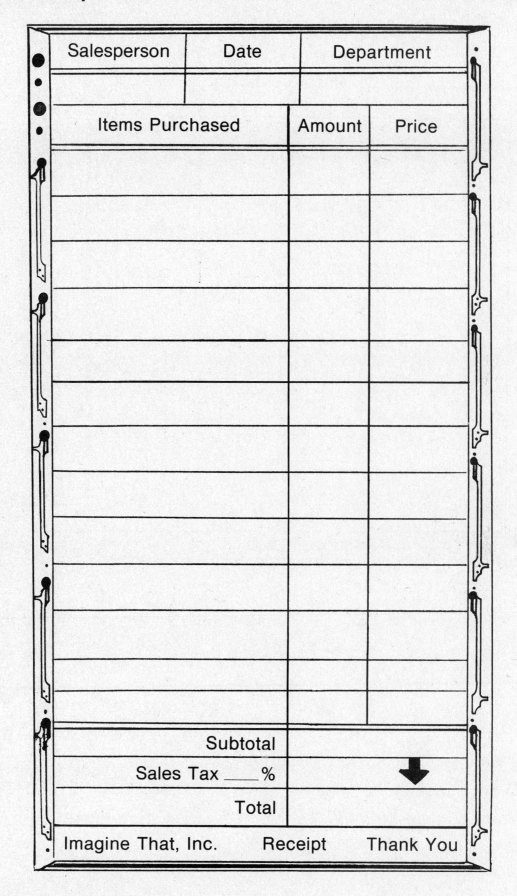

Salesperson	Date	Department

Items Purchased	Amount	Price
Subtotal		
Sales Tax ____%		
Total		
Imagine That, Inc.	Receipt	Thank You

For specific instructions see page 87

Mirror Image

My Mirror Image

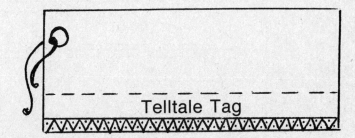

Telltale Tag

1. Draw a face in the mirror.
2. Write one word on the Telltale Tag to describe the face.

For specific instructions see page 93

Stepping-Stones

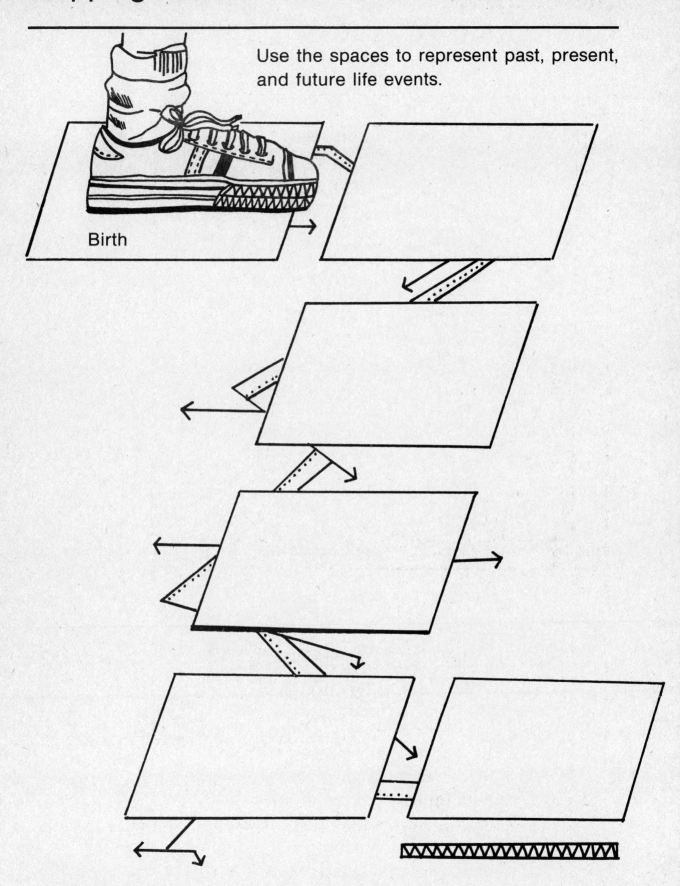

Use the spaces to represent past, present, and future life events.

Birth

For specific instructions see page 97

Grumpy T-Shirt

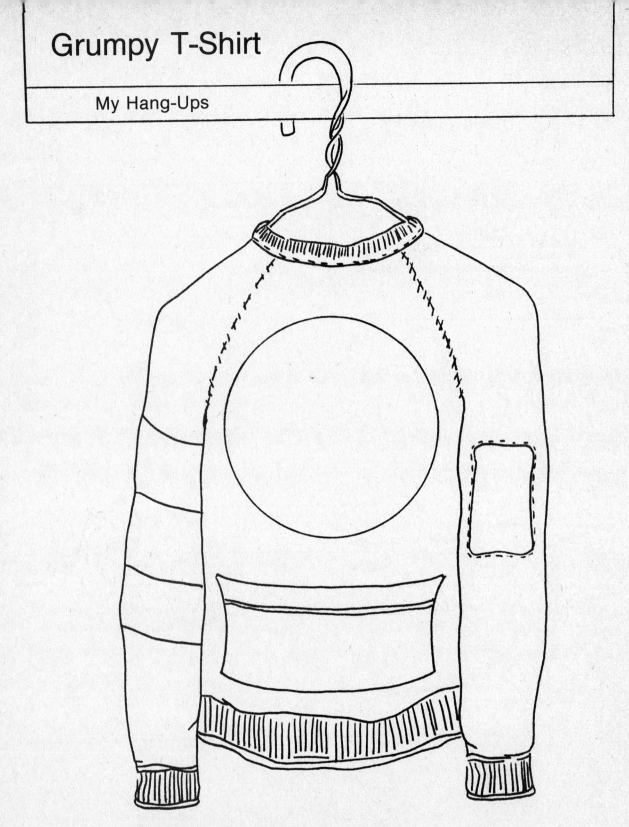

Design your own Grumpy T-Shirt:
1. Draw a grumpy picture in the circle.
2. Write a grumpy sentence on the front pocket.
3. Write a grumpy number on the patch on the sleeve.
4. Choose two grumpy colors for the stripes on the sleeve.

For specific instructions see page 106

Sure Cure

Diagnosis

Consultation

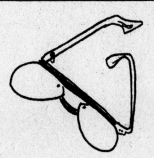

Prescription

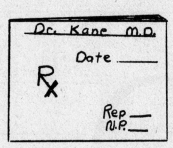

Cure

For specific instructions see page 113

I Always Remember

I Always Forget

For specific instructions see page 118

Lazy Language

Take your lazy feelings on a walk.

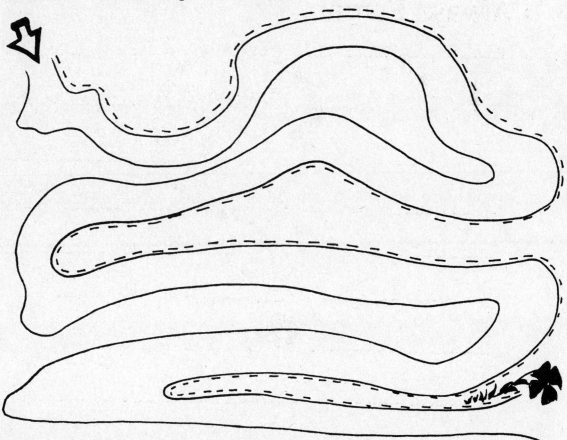

For specific instructions see page 121